# ENTREPRENEURIAL INTELLIGENCE

## INSPIRED BY THE PHILOSOPHIES OF COFFEE ENTREPRENEUR
### *Phillip Di Bella*

# ALLAN BONSALL

Esstee Media

West End

Brisbane

Entrepreneurial Intelligence
Copyright©Allan Bonsall 2014


National Library of Australia Cataloguing-in-Publication entry

Entrepreneurial intelligence : inspired by the philosophies  of coffee
entrepreneur Phillip Di Bella

ISBN:        9780975816790 (paperback)

Dewey Number:    658.421



Published by Allan Bonsall
in association with:
Esstee Media
West End
Queensland
ABN 99 364 832 591
www.essteemedia.com

Edited by Stephen Thompson
Layout by Esstee Media
Cover design by Kevin Fielding
Cover photography by Peter Mylonas
Artwork by Leslie Robinson

# Contents

# Foreword

by Phillip Di Bella

## "Turning entrepreneurial thinkers into entrepreneurial doers"

Not long after we began this journey, Gianna and I spent some time with Richard Branson on Necker Island. When we returned to Australia, friends and colleagues were curious and full of questions. Not surprisingly, as Branson is one of the most respected and successful entrepreneurs currently walking the planet. A week or so later, I was scheduled to have a discussion with Allan Bonsall about the progress of this book. We talked at length about the role of vision and what the concept of visioning meant to me. After a short break, Allan asked who inspired me. We had discussed my meetings with Branson. Did someone like Branson inspire me? Did people like Bill Gates or Steve Jobs, maybe Muhammad Ali inspire me? The answer I gave him was probably not the answer he expected.

I believe that 80% of my inspiration has to come from within. I also believe that that is my greatest strength. I don't deny that there are other people who inspire me. My children inspire me; when I watch them learn something new I am incredibly inspired by what human beings are capable of achieving. But if I allow my inspiration to be someone like Richard Branson, then I run the risk of simply imitating Branson, and if I copy Branson then how do I benchmark my own performance? If my inspiration is me, then I am not copying anyone and the only benchmark that is important is the one I set myself.

On the other hand, I am passionate about learning. Every time I read something new or listen to a success story, I am looking for some little bit of gold dust that I can take away. I will pick up a book like this, and if I find two things that add value to my journey then it has been a worthwhile investment of my time. I came away from Necker Island with an amazing insight from Branson that I used to focus my own team when I returned. For me, learning is a constant thing in my life, not just something that I set down as an agenda item for today or tomorrow. But there is also a responsibility that comes with learning – if you learn it and don't share it, you waste it.

Learning and understanding are different outcomes than being inspired. There are speakers out there delivering so-called inspirational and motivational seminars. Some of them are household names known across the globe, but the product they're selling is not success; their business is public speaking, and the only people in that business who get wealthy are the motivators themselves. I decided a long time ago that I would donate every cent I got from public speaking to charity. That way I'm not compromised in what I want to achieve, and there is no expectation on me to falsely inspire or to motivate for the wrong reason, or for mistaken hope.

Whenever I stand up in front of an audience and look across the expectant faces in front of me I focus on the prospective entrepreneurs in the audience; more specifically, the people who would be intelligent entrepreneurs. There is no doubt in my mind that the people who will apply entrepreneurial intelligence are the same people who understand that their inspiration must come from within. For those people in the audience who have come only to be inspired, the people who are searching for 80% of their inspiration outside of themselves, those people will never succeed.

I have a very simple expectation from this book, and it is this: if we can motivate people who may be entrepreneurial thinkers to become entrepreneurial doers then it has all been worthwhile. If I can assist them in that quest then I will be very happy. If, by sharing my story, other people can be motivated to dig inside themselves and find their own passion, dig inside themselves and create their own vision, then I will definitely believe that this effort has been worthwhile.

A special thank you to Gianna for sharing this great journey; living and working with an entrepreneur cannot be easy, and her patience and calmness amazes me. My wife, and my beautiful children, Arnika and Ali, have taught me so much and inspire me to become better at everything I do.

To my team in Australia and internationally, thank you for your dedication, your loyalty and the commitment you give to making the Di Bella brand world-class.

Finally, it would be remiss of me not to congratulate Allan Bonsall on telling this story so brilliantly. His determination to both entertain and inform is a reward in itself. Not only has he captured my thoughts and beliefs but, at the same time, he has flattered me with the company I have shared throughout.

**Phillip  Di Bella**

# Acknowledgements

A small group of people had a hand in bringing this project to a satisfactory conclusion.

A very special thank you to Gianna Di Bella, Phillip's wife and partner in the business. Not only has Gianna provided unwavering support for the project, she has also helped me enormously with constructive advice and review of the manuscript as it has unfolded. (Phillip announced very early in the piece that he trusted Gianna to be his objective other self.)

I also want to thank Kevin Fielding, a creative genius whose inspired design for the front cover will hopefully capture the attention of every budding entrepreneur in the land.

My thanks also to Stephen Thompson, who undertook the thankless task of charting the maze when the writing was finished, and when the hard work begins to get every writer's masterpiece into the waiting hands of an expectant audience.

I should also thank Phillip Di Bella for his patience. At every opportunity over the past year, Phillip has spruiked the book, saying that it is nearly finished. At least now he will be telling his audience the truth.

And, finally, a heartfelt thank you to Jann, my wife, who for the past couple of years has had to suffer the mood swings and the frustrated outbursts of a perfectionist.

# Preface

Different people define success in different ways. One of the most insightful definitions I've heard recently is that success equals freedom; freedom to do what you want to do, achieve what you want to achieve and be what you want to be. Others have defined success as wealth, while many spurn wealth and point to satisfaction and achievement. However you define success, the bottom line is clear: wealth provides the capacity to make it happen, to enable the level of freedom we all aspire to, but which very few really achieve.

There are two fundamental ways to build wealth. One is through opportunity, such as real estate or the resource sector; the other is through creating wealth on an idea, or a skill. While there are a huge number of start-up companies in property development or resource exploration, many more emerge through the second category; the best motor mechanic in the dealership splits to set up his own workshop (skill); a young retail whiz sees the opportunity to set up an online store to service a niche market (idea); a seasoned ad man sees the opportunity to build an agency around a lucrative client (skill and idea).

In Australia, only 50% of these start-up companies will be operational in 10 years' time. Some make it big, most don't; many others crash and burn. The question is, why? What makes the difference between amazing success, and dismal failure?

Making this question even more compelling is the significance these statistics have on the overall strength of a country. Each year more than 20,000 new companies are set up in Australia. They are the launching pad of most of the world's economy, and the genesis of every one is an entrepreneur who started out with a dream and made it happen.

What drives the success of entrepreneurs like Britain's Branson, America's Gates, India's Lakshmi Millat, Sweden's Ingvar Kamprad, Mexico's Carlos Slim Helu, Russia's Roman Abramovich or Australia's Dick Smith and Janine Allis? Why did these entrepreneurs achieve success at a young age when most people struggle through their lives with little to show for it? Are these people blessed with something that mere mortals don't have; an ability to translate everything they do into wealth and success?

Recently I attended a forum of young, budding entrepreneurs. I was there at the invitation of Phillip Di Bella, the founder of Di Bella Coffee. At the age of 38, Phillip has kicked more goals than most of us will achieve in a lifetime. He began Di Bella Coffee in 2002 with just AUD$5000 in his pocket. Within 4 years his company had made BRW's Top 100 Fastest Growing list and Phillip was named in the top 100 young rich. In 2005 he was a finalist in Ernst & Young's Young Entrepreneur of the Year and went on to win in 2008. Three years later, Phillip and his wife Gianna were listed in Queensland's top 100 rich lists, the same year Phillip was appointed an adjunct professor in entrepreneurship at Griffith University.

Phillip had asked me to join him at the forum of young entrepreneurs to be part of a small panel of 'masters' to share our life experiences with the 70 or 80 predominantly Gen Ys in the audience.

This amazing word 'entrepreneur' seems to draw people like a magnet. They come in all shapes and sizes, from an amazing array of backgrounds and with varying levels of formal education. Without doubt they all share one common goal: to succeed, and for almost every one of them, success is generally spelt with an E for entrepreneurship.

What made this event even more compelling was that everyone there had given up precious time on a weekend to attend.

As the day unfolded, an intriguing diversity became clear within the group. A handful of people were already running successful ventures, including one entrepreneur who was achieving fantastic results designing and selling bikinis online. Several others had established successful marketing agencies across a gamut of products and services.

A slightly larger group of people had a reasonably clear picture of what they wanted to achieve, and were well advanced in developing their plans. What they needed was, perhaps, a little extra push, or a small dose of inspiration to help get them over the line.

By far the largest number of people at the forum had no clear picture of what they wanted to do, or much of an idea about how they would achieve it. At times they appeared uncomfortable, out of their depth. At other times they seemed unsure how to translate what they were hearing into something tangible they could use.

And, finally, there was another, fortunately quite small, group of people who could well represent the most concerning aspect of the entrepreneurship bubble: those that came along in the hope that a little of the entrepreneurial magic dust of people like Phillip Di Bella might just rub off on them.

This is the conundrum and the dream all rolled into one. For many, to simply be an entrepreneur is both the way and the how; that if you can somehow achieve the status of entrepreneurship, then that will magically conjure up a yellow brick road to untold wealth and glory.

We can be sure that almost every one of the young people at that forum has at some time picked up a book about entrepreneurship. For some, what they have read may have consolidated a belief, or reaffirmed a commitment. Others may have been inspired to start their journey without really having a roadmap to finish it. Most agree that they are yet to find a book that provides them with a framework clearly articulating what is required to become a successful entrepreneur, and what is missing in those who fail. The brilliant simplicity of Branson's mantra of "Just do it" may actually leave aspiring entrepreneurs lost when it comes to the question of 'do what?' To be inspired is one thing, to understand the 'how' is another thing entirely.

Phillip Di Bella is quick to dispel the notion that somehow his success is the result of being exposed to magic entrepreneurial dust. He agrees that most authors on the subject struggle to articulate what it really means to be an entrepreneur, to achieve success as an entrepreneur, how to translate the dream into reality, or how to turn the wishful magical entrepreneurial dust into tangible outcomes.

So, is there a formula that enables entrepreneurs to create wealth, something that combines tangible traits with, perhaps, a number of intangibles? Is it a combination of smart business practices, a strong work ethic and a commitment to persevering even when the odds are frighteningly against you? Does a formula exist that a budding entrepreneur can apply when setting out in business, with a view to that business growing and growing and growing? And if there is such a formula, is it possible to articulate it in a way that everyone can understand?

Phillip Di Bella and I believe there is, and that it is a surprisingly simple formula capable of providing a new and enlightened way of looking at entrepreneurship and to understand what it is that makes entrepreneurs successful. It is a formula that acknowledges the tangible with the intangible of entrepreneurial thinking, a formula that builds on the customer-centric driver that all entrepreneurs acknowledge. It is an idea that we have called **Entrepreneurial Intelligence**.

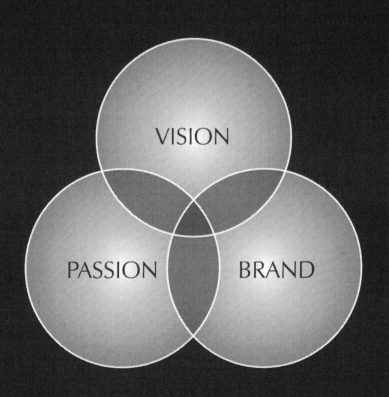

# 1

# Vision, Passion, Brand

The weather forecast was for another perfect autumn day in Brisbane. The heat of the summer had made way for cooler nights, less humidity making sleep easier. It's close to 4:30 a.m. on the second Saturday in April, 2003, and Phillip Di Bella has just dragged himself out of bed.

He splashes water on his face, pulls the covers over the bed in the converted office he's using as a bedroom and walks down the rickety staircase into the warehouse. He's surrounded by the remnants of the week's roasting and packing, but the van is already loaded; he'd made sure of that before collapsing into bed the night before. He looks around him, at his office, his workplace and his home, the place where he spends most of his time when he's not seeing customers. Not the most salubrious place in the world, he acknowledges to himself grabbing the chain of the massive roller door, but it will do for the moment.

Ten minutes later, he pulls up in front of an old power station in New Farm. Abandoned due to rising costs in the 1970s, the Powerhouse has been reborn as a cultural centre and venue for Brisbane's performing artists, and is home, every second and fourth Saturday of the month, to Jan Power's popular Farmers' Markets. At this early hour the place is already a hive of activity. Farmers and artisans, bakers and butchers and an eclectic assortment of traders follow well-practised set-up procedures to transform the footpath snaking between New Farm Park and the massive concrete structure into a food lover's paradise.

Phillip sets up his mobile coffee cart next to a baker's stall. The aroma of freshly baked bread from his neighbour's baskets gets the juices running in his mouth. He quickens his pace, laying out the tools of his trade, making sure everything he needs is close to hand. Soon the aroma of roasted coffee beans will be swirling through the air, mingling with all the other smells that entice and delight the locals and visitors who flock to the market. There is banter between the old hands, cries of good morning, a sudden burst of laughter. Phillip's neighbour nods, but then turns to the task at hand. Although personally invited by Jan Power to be part of the market, Phillip is still the new boy on the block, largely ignored by the regulars, intent as they are on their own endeavours to set-up.

Jan Power is a Brisbane icon, highly respected for her entrepreneurial pursuits and a well-known and oft quoted media favourite. To have a personal invitation from Jan was not only flattering, but an enormous opportunity. The Farmers' Markets are not what Phillip defines as core business; he sees his future as a roaster and a wholesaler, and his primary market as the owners of cafes and restaurants. The Farmers' Markets are unashamedly retail, but they represent a golden opportunity to get close to the people Phillip knows will be the lifeblood of his company if he can convince them to become loyal supporters of the Di Bella Brand. These are the people who will ensure his ultimate success; they are the customers of his customers, the people who frequent the cafes and restaurants for a quality caffeine fix.

This is Phillip's fifth time at the markets. The first four occasions had been lean affairs and it would have been easy for him to conclude he was wasting his time. Perhaps someone without less single-minded focus may have already pulled out. But Phillip was determined to make the most of this opportunity.

It is only just light, the sun still yet to show itself above the trees and buildings flanking the marketplace. Even in the gloom the gold, black and white Di Bella Coffee logo looks polished and alive. Next door, Phillip can see the baker moving between several customers; the baker's wife materialises from the rear of their stall and is immediately in the fray. Against a lightening sky, a trickle of people move from one vendor to the next. Phillip is ready, only the beans wait to be ground to ensure absolute freshness. How long, he wonders, will it be before the first caffeine fix is sought out by one of the early birds?

People walk past, their eyes watching the ground, or looking ahead to seek out their favourite stall for the delights they are keen to share with family and friends over the weekend. Phillip waits patiently, but no one stops. Slowly, the sun climbs in the morning sky with the promise of it being much hotter than the bureau had predicted. By 9 am only twelve people have stopped to order a coffee; by midday, as the market heads towards a close, Phillip Di Bella has sold a total of fifty-four cappuccinos, twenty-one lattes and four short blacks – a disappointing result, perhaps.

Phillip Di Bella packs up his cart and goes looking for Jan Power. When he sees her, she is engaged in an animated discussion with a number of stall-holders clearly unhappy about something. Two of the men are competing with each other to gain Power's attention. Each one gesticulates dramatically with hands and arms, loudly talking over one another. Phillip turns and walks back to his cart. He is smiling to himself. By his guess, the disappointed stall-holders will be keeping Jan Power occupied for a while so he may as well head back to home and the warehouse, he would send her an e-mail to thank her and tell her how pleased he is.

This had been his best day so far. The numbers were disappointing, to a point, but they were almost half again on the previous Saturday. More importantly, the people who had stopped to try his coffee had given him some market intelligence, which was priceless.

The ones who stopped were clearly passionate about their

coffee. He had recognised some as repeat customers. They had complimented him on the quality of his roast and wanted to know who his supplier was. Proudly, he'd told them he roasted and blended his own. The discerning coffee drinkers were impressed and had asked if he would be back. Without hesitation, Phillip assured them he would be.

I tell this story because I believe it contains most of the clues necessary to gain a better insight into what we mean by entrepreneurial intelligence. It begins with the most fundamental of business principles: to place the customer at the very heart, at the very core of a venture. This is a principle that we will constantly return to as our story unfolds, in ways which will hopefully enlighten and provide guidance.

Do a bit of digging, however, and it becomes clear that all successful entrepreneurs share several other common traits. Their commitment is obvious, so is a preparedness to work hard. But commitment and hard work aren't scarce commodities or attributes. At some point, most people will show commitment above and beyond the norm, and preparedness to work hard is not lacking in most of us.

So what is it that these people, including Phillip Di Bella, have been blessed with that others haven't? More to the point, what do they attribute their success to?

Richard Branson, the very flamboyant British entrepreneur, demonstrates an insatiable appetite for starting new ventures. Since setting up Virgin Records in 1972, Branson has gone on to build dozens of different businesses, including airlines, publishing houses, credit cards, trains, holiday ventures and megastores. He even launched the first galactic adventure for paying customers. He has enjoyed many successes, but he has also suffered a number of well-publicised failures. His work ethic is beyond question; far from being daunted by the workload, he thrives on it. Without doubt, Branson looks at business in his own unique way. "Business has to be involving, it has to be fun, and it has to exercise your creative instincts." So, perhaps entrepreneurial success for Branson is perseverance with a healthy dose of fun.

Australia's Gerry Harvey, co-owner of Harvey Norman, is no shirker, and his commitment cannot be doubted. "I went to the brink many times," he is quoted as saying in his own inimitable way. "A couple of times I thought: I'm gone ... this is it. But then you would just keep working. I think if you're close to the brink ... just make sure that you work twice as hard and put twice as much effort into everything and ... you should come through."

Twice as much effort, is that the secret to Gerry Harvey's formula for success? Clearly it touches on a number of the man's key strengths, but does it amount to his complete mantra? We doubt it.

Steve Jobs once wrapped up Apple's success in this simple statement: "I think we're having fun. I think our customers really like our products. And we're always trying to do better." Like Branson and Harvey, Jobs wasn't frightened of hard work, because to him work was fun. Sure there is a large measure of commitment in trying to do better, but again, is trying harder the secret formula? Or was his point more about being customer-centric, by placing customers at the heart of the business? Was that his formula for success?

Apple has become one of the world's most powerful brands, consistently ranking in the global top three. Ironically it was a golfing entrepreneur, Greg Norman, who suggested that his success was about the brand. He argued that "our success is a direct result of knowing how to market a brand and having the right people representing the brand." No argument there from the brand strategists, but again, we question whether this is his complete formula for success.

John Ilhan, the founder of Crazy Johns who tragically passed away at 42, argued that his success was in the numbers: "It's a very tough market. So unless you do a really good job, you buy the right products from the manufacturers, you service the customer, they keep coming back, they bring their friends in, it's all about the numbers, numbers, numbers." Ilhan also talked about customer service and sound purchasing practices, but at the end of the day was Ilhan's success about volume, or something else?

Phillip Di Bella's formula for entrepreneurial success connects with each of the touch-points I have already described, but then it adds an intriguing dimension. Phillip holds a bachelor degree and has been appointed an adjunct professor in entrepreneurship at Griffith University. He is very proud of both achievements, but Phillip is probably the furthest thing from an academic that you will ever find.

He is largely self-taught and has a voracious appetite for knowledge. He consumes books on business philosophy, leadership and trust, books about self-achievers, successful men and women in all walks of life. He reads them, takes from them what he believes adds value to his own needs and then discards them. Time is always the enemy, and to satisfy his appetite he has taken to audio-books in a big way. I gave him a hard-back copy of Steve Jobs' biography by Walter Isaacson as a must read, and he quipped back, "do you have the audio book?"

Regardless of the medium, Phillip Di Bella is a voracious consumer of ideas and better ways to kick goals. He acknowledges the people who have mentored and guided him, and the ideas that inspire him. He has never arrogantly assumed that he has all the answers. But he has a natural talent for lining up all the ducks in a row so they make sense.

Some of the most successful formulas in the world have been discovered by accident. One element accidently mixed with another creates an explosion, and dynamite is discovered. Biologists introduce three cells to each other on a petri dish, a shallow cylindrical dish used for experiments, and nothing happens. A fourth cell is introduced, and suddenly the first cell teams up with the second and third and together they begin eating the fourth, and a powerful medical discovery is made. Without the fourth, the first three have a function, but it is not enough to create a new function. Introduce the final part to the formula and the dynamic becomes a world beater. The formula for intelligent entrepreneurship works the same way.

Imagine if you will a Venn diagram that lays out for you the formula for entrepreneurial success. The simplicity of a Venn diagram as a series of interconnecting circles on the same plane works well for this purpose. Each circle represents a key part of the formula, while the overlaps connect the parts to each other and reinforce the connectivity between all the parts.

In our Venn diagram there are three fundamental parts of the Entrepreneurial Intelligence Formula, three things all successful entrepreneurs appear to demonstrate consistently. The three parts can be summarised easily with three simple words: **Vision**, **Passion** and **Brand**.

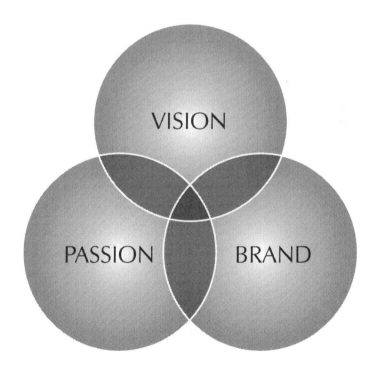

**Vision** is the foundation on which every great entrepreneur will build their success. Not some warm and fuzzy vision statement that you often see on the walls of self-important and self-obsessed corporations, talking about integrity, honesty and the American way. What we're talking about is the ability of an individual to define a purpose, a goal, a personal agenda, or even a legacy that they want to achieve, and then be able to share that vision with others so that it grows. In its simplest, purest form, vision refers to a future place that every successful entrepreneur can see clearly in their head. This vision must be powerful enough to arouse and sustain the entrepreneur's motivation and to drive the actions necessary for it to become a reality.

When Phillip Di Bella accepted Jan Power's invitation to sell coffee at the Farmers' Markets he was deliberately stepping away from his primary customers, but he was not forsaking the vision he had spelled out for himself. Key to that vision was a customer experience that he could control, one which was not driven by the vagaries and discounting mentality of the mass retail sector. For that reason there were no supermarkets or convenience stores in Phillip's vision, and there still aren't. Phillip's focus was to build a strategy around opportunities for the most discerning consumers to experience, to delight in, and then to share what Phillip describes as "the ultimate coffee experience".

In the beginning, the only way he was prepared to guarantee that experience was through the best quality restaurants and the most fashionable and trendsetting cafes, the owners of which were also entrepreneurs, men and women who were equally concerned about the satisfaction of their customers' experience.

***

The next part of the formula we believe all successful entrepreneurs' demonstrate is **Passion**. Without passion we don't believe you will ever achieve your ultimate goal of success.

Consider each of the people we discussed in the Preface to this book and ask yourself: are they exhibiting passion in their endeavours? If your answer is a tentative yes, or maybe, then perhaps this book is not really for you. On the other hand, if your answer is a resounding yes, then the next question follows automatically: passion about what? And in order to understand the 'what', we need to explore how to define each person's passion, and then to identify how it is manifested?

On the surface, it would be easy to think of Phillip Di Bella's commitment and perseverance at Jan Power's Farmers' Markets as passion. Of course, it is, but it's not the only layer of passion we're trying to understand here. Commitment and energy, as we will discuss, are parts of a successful entrepreneur's passion, but they can't, and don't, define it. Phillip's decision to work 120 hour weeks, and his preparedness to buy a warehouse, which became both his place of work and his residence, are examples of his determination to succeed. Clearly that is a part of the man's passion. But so was his decision to use the markets to explore customer's attitudes. That was both a demonstration of his passion to succeed and his passion in getting the product experience right.

Passion is not a one-dimensional concept. There is no single rule that you can use to pigeonhole passion and say, there, that's how my passion manifests itself. If it were that easy, there would be no need for a book such as this.

Passion envelops us all. It is the most intense of emotions, a compelling feeling or enthusiasm that can consume us when we want to achieve something, or when we desire something. Kicking goals is a huge motivator for entrepreneurs. When it happens, passion is there in its purest sense because it is all consuming. It may be that your own passion is there at the very outset, from the starting blocks of your journey, such as a hobby or a very personal driving interest, such as a social wrong, or a decision to commit your life to protecting the environment. You may discover passion as you embark on the journey, when something you had a passing interest in becomes an obsession. You may have had a passion for sport, which has transformed into a passion to succeed on a broader landscape than just your youthful energy on the football field or netball court.

When it comes to discovering your passion, there is one fact that will be clear, that will overwhelm you when you find it. Passion is the life-force of your ambition; without it you might climb someway up the ladder, but without passion you will never get to the top.

\*\*\*

The third part of the formula and the third attribute that every great entrepreneur demonstrates is, perhaps, more tangible than vision or passion, because it has to be. The third part of the formula is an innate understanding of, and the ability to harness, the power of their **Brand**.

Far too many people view the idea of a brand from a very narrow perspective. Branded consumer goods, like Apple, Nike and Coca-Cola are readily identified as brands by what people see as the brand markings – the logo, the packaging and the advertising. In this context the brand is often viewed as a one-dimensional aspect of the marketing function and can be easily dismissed by the narrow-minded, a very dangerous and a very misleading presumption that couldn't be further from reality.

The potential power of brand has only been truly acknowledged in recent times. Stephen King, an English adman, not the acclaimed writer of horror fiction, highlighted this power when he compared the complexity of the brand with the limitations of an unbranded product:

"A product is something that is made in a factory; a brand is something that is bought by a customer. A product can be copied by a competitor; a brand is unique. A product can be quickly outdated; a successful brand is timeless."

Successful entrepreneurs never underestimate the power of their brand. They understand that their brand is the most powerful link they have with their customers. Successful entrepreneurs intuitively know that their brand is the key to building loyalty and generating repeat purchase and referral.

In the following pages we will examine each of the parts that make up the formula for intelligent entrepreneurial success: how they work, why they work, and how you can make them work for you. That's the mission of this book – not to dispel the myths as such, but to put some understanding and clarity around what it takes to be an entrepreneur, and to provide you with clear and purposeful steps on how to apply entrepreneurial intelligence.

But, before we do so, there is one final ingredient in the formula that we cannot ignore, an ingredient which belongs in a very special place in every Venn diagram.

Each of the circles that make up a Venn diagram is created equal regardless of where it sits. No single part of the formula dominates the others. In our diagram, Vision is positioned at the top, but rotate the diagram in a clockwise direction and suddenly Passion sits at the top. Rotate them again and Brand assumes that position. Regardless of which part appears to be dominant, the real power of a Venn diagram lies in the overlaps, which inextricably link each key component to the other. Vision is linked to Brand, and in that overlap are the disciplines and actions that must co-exist between the two parts for success. In the same way, Brand is linked to Passion, and Passion to Vision. Each of the overlaps defines the relationship between the parts. As we rotate the key parts, in a demonstration of equality, the overlaps move with them. And at the very heart of the diagram, the place where the three parts have their strongest link, is one overlap that binds all three parts together. In our formula, that critical overlap is defined as 'the other EI', perhaps a better known combination of the two letters "E" and "I" – **Emotional Intelligence.**

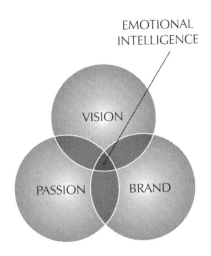

On the black acrylic notice board in his office, Phillip Di Bella tracks the progress of senior management against the company's strategic plan. In one corner of the board he keeps a reminder for himself, and for his directors, of the importance of the final ingredient in the formula for intelligent entrepreneurship. It is there on the board to remind everyone that almost every decision they take, every strategy they initiate, will ultimately need to engage with what is known around the globe as EQ or EI.

Many credit Daniel Goleman with developing the concept of EI and writing the book on emotional intelligence that the business world has claimed as its own philosophy. Since the phenomenal success of EI, businesses across the globe have incorporated emotional intelligence into almost every aspect of business function. But, in doing so, they have come very close to abusing the original concept.

The Harvard Business Review hailed EI as a "ground breaking, paradigm shattering idea" and one of the most influential business ideas of the 90s. Goleman has subsequently tried to set the record straight by criticising some of the over-heated claims others have made about EI, but nothing can change the fundamental value of emotional intelligence.

Simply put, EI is an individual's ability to be both aware of their own emotions and the emotions of those around them. It is the capacity great entrepreneurs have to engage with people in a way that recognises and prioritises the needs of others, often subjugating their own ambitions in the process.

EI provides those engaged with entrepreneurial intelligence with both a timely reminder and a powerful resource. Ironically, both come from the same examination of leadership ability and capacity. The timely reminder is that great leaders register high levels of EI, while the idea of EI as a resource is that EI is not an inherited skill or trait. EI can be learnt. To discover how, you will need to keep reading.

This brings us to the question of where to embark on this journey towards entrepreneurial intelligence. Try to discuss the three core components democratically and it becomes an intriguing debate driven by individual preference or partiality. Introduce the capacity of EI to add value to each part and the discussion about where to start becomes even more complex, because each part of the formula is intrinsically linked to the other without any one appearing to be the driver.

Of course there is logic to where to start. Everything in this world must have a beginning, including the world. Every inventor starts out with a reasonable hypothesis even if their ultimate discovery is something else entirely. So I will start where the successful entrepreneurs start, with a vision of what they see.

While you are reading, remember the biologists who began their simple experiment in the petri dish by introducing three cells. By itself, each cell had a valuable function, able to be defined and understood. When the biologists introduced a fourth cell they created something infinitely more valuable than the sum total of the four parts; they created something that was powerful enough to change the world. The lesson is very simple. Don't be fooled into thinking that your passion will cover a lack of vision, or that your brand will make up for shortcomings in passion, or that once you have clearly articulated your vision and applied the right level of EI, that you can take the afternoon off. For the entrepreneurial intelligence formula to work, you must get all the parts right; three out of four just won't cut it.

It is up to you to determine whether you have the desire to apply entrepreneurial intelligence. Like the forum of young budding entrepreneurs I attended with Phillip Di Bella, there are many with the hunger to succeed who simply need some kind of road map, or something that will just nudge their confidence in the right direction. Others may require more of a push. That is what this book is all about.

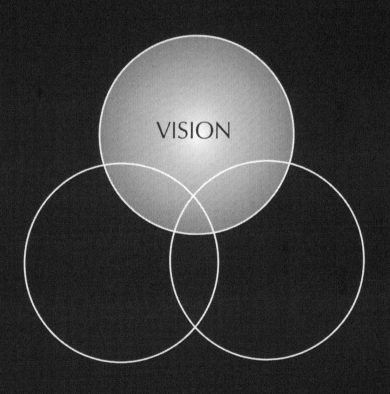

# 2

# This thing called Vision

When Lewis Carroll wrote *Through the Looking-glass* in 1872 he captured the essence of an idea that has been explored by many since. In a simple exchange between Alice and the Cheshire Cat, Carroll indelibly marked out the dilemma that every budding entrepreneur must confront.

> Alice: Which way should I go?
> Cat: That depends on where you are going.
> Alice: I don't know where I'm going!
> Cat: Then it doesn't much matter which way you go![1]

For Phillip Di Bella, this is always the nub of the dilemma.

"If you don't know where you want to go, it makes little difference if you make no progress in getting there."

He quickly adds that knowing where you want to go should not be a complex or complicated notion, or that there is a single or right way to define it:

---

1    Carroll, Lewis (1872) *Through the Looking Glass*, London: Macmillan.

"A vision can be a short, succinct statement of three words, or a single sentence, or a series of ideas. The question of how long a vision is misses the point. Great wordsmiths can write a ten-line sentence using only commas and colons and still bring the sentence to life. But for what purpose, if it doesn't describe what your vision means to you?"

Phillip sees the process of envisioning a future place as the simplest thing on earth.

"Vision is what you see. My vision is what I see." (He emphasises the point by tapping his chest). "What I see, not what someone else sees, or doesn't see. So when I started Di Bella Coffee I had a clear picture in my head of Di Bella Coffee in cafes and restaurants across the country. I didn't see it in supermarkets; I didn't see it in petrol stations or convenience outlets. I saw it where people would be able to enjoy a perfect cup of coffee every time they visited."

If envisioning a future place is as simple as we suggest why hasn't the idea of creating a vision swept the business world? Why do people run hot and cold on the importance of setting a vision? Why do so few owners of start-up companies in this country devise a vision of what the company will be in the future?

You often hear the expression SME, or small medium enterprise, associated with these start-up companies. By itself, the definition is simply a statement of size. A small company is defined by the Australian Bureau of Statistics as a company with up to 19 employees, and is generally the starting point for most entrepreneurs. This presents us with an intriguing, yet senseless, dichotomy. Evidence shows that very few people who start up a new company develop a vision for their future, yet it would be foolhardy to believe that any budding entrepreneur starts out with the ambition of remaining a small enterprise.

Unfortunately, that is exactly what happens, with in excess of 80% of all businesses in Australia defined as small.

Compounding the lack of vision in most SMEs is the high level of cynicism surrounding the 'vision' concept. Critics describe the vision statements hanging in company foyers as nothing more than framed reminders to recalcitrant employees, urging them to give their all to making the company's shareholders richer than they already are. Each time our leaders and politicians fail to articulate a vision, or fail to deliver on a vision they have promised, we immediately start to question the veracity of visioning in the first place.

Perhaps the primary reason why the concept of visioning has failed to take hold is not in the definition, but in the failure of people to sell the concept. As any exponent of the craft of advertising will tell you, the higher the level of cynicism or negative perception, the harder you have to work at changing people's minds.

In the selling of the idea of vision, we are convinced that the authors and the exponents have simply made it too hard.

The simplicity Phillip Di Bella talks about is missing when you go looking for a clear, concise definition through the pages of business books. While authors agree that Visions and Mission Statements are compulsory components of strategic or business planning, all too often the same authors confront the reader with a maze of cleverly disguised rhetoric that fails to ignite the imagination.

Read any book on strategic planning and you will be confronted by what appears to be an unnecessarily high level of process. The language is dry and unemotional: situation analysis, priority issues, vision, mission statement, objectives, strategies, program development, delegation, accountability and review. That the language is focused is beyond question, but to what advantage if the appeal is like an empty water bottle in the middle of the Sahara Desert?

Google 'vision statement' or its close companion 'mission statement' and you will be overwhelmed with variations of the same basic concept of what constitutes a vision, or what comprises a mission. Most will define a vision as a statement about what the organisation or company wants to look like in the future; while mission, they will contend, refers to what the organisation is doing to get there.

While they are all overwhelmingly right, we are caught up in a trap of our own making in which the consultants and planners who write the books on visioning and strategic planning need you to believe they are the experts. They go to great lengths to expand on their theories, to provide exhaustive detail on the component parts of each step you need to take. A SWOT analysis becomes a complex formula rivalling the great mathematicians, risk assessment goes beyond the necessary and drills down to the effect the nuclear stand-off between Israel and Iran will have on your business - and the simple idea of a vision is swept up in the vortex.

What the experts don't tell you is that the process of strategic planning is deceptively simple and can be explained in three parts: where are we now, where do we want to be, and how will we get there.

But, and it is a big but, before you can determine the 'how' you must first define 'where' you want to be, and as Phillip Di Bella put it so succinctly, only you can create that vision because your "vision is what you see. What you want to achieve – what you believe you can achieve."

One of the most talked about visions of all time came into being fifty years ago in the United States. It was a vision shared by millions, but it was one man's vision of a future place; what this one man could see and what this one man believed could happen.

Martin Luther King was a preacher, someone who was comfortable with abstract ideas and concepts. He saw nothing incongruous about the values of a God that no one has seen or can define in any way other than as a belief. As a youngster, King questioned some of the teachings of *The Bible*; at one point he strenuously denied the Christian belief in Jesus Christ's resurrection.

Still, it was clear that his heart was already set on a particular path when he conceded that *The Bible* contained too many truths to be disregarded.

By all accounts, he was a precocious and talented student who gained entry into university at the age of 15. He graduated with a Bachelor of Arts degree in sociology, and immediately enrolled in Crozer Theological Seminary, Philadelphia, graduating with a Bachelor of Divinity. At 25 he was appointed pastor of the Dexter Avenue Baptist Church, Montgomery, Alabama. He continued studying and received a Doctorate of Philosophy from Boston University a few years later.

His thoughts and ideas were shaped by a diversity of experiences. He was inspired by Mahatma Gandhi, and visited the great Indian leader's birthplace. The trip had a profound effect on King. It reaffirmed his belief in non-violent resistance, while consolidating his determination to focus his energy on America's struggle for civil rights.

Not surprisingly his views brought with them a degree of celebrity and notoriety. He became a target of the FBI because of his outspoken ways, and was subjected to intense scrutiny of his private life in attempts to discredit him and his beliefs.

Martin Luther King Jnr was, in all aspects of his life, a charismatic leader and a visionary, and on the 28th of August 1963 he stood on the steps of the Lincoln Memorial, in Washington D.C., and made a speech which electrified the crowd before him.

More than a quarter of a million people had assembled in Washington to protest the desperate conditions of black Americans in the southern states, and to embarrass the government for its failure to safeguard the civil rights of blacks.

Martin Luther King was only one of a number of speakers scheduled to address the crowd, but when he talked about his vision to end racial segregation in the United States you could have heard a pin drop.

"I have a dream that one day on the red hills of Georgia, the sons of the former slaves and the sons of the former slave owners will be able to sit down together at the table of brotherhood.

I have a dream that one day even the state of Mississippi, a desert state sweltering with the heat of injustice and oppression, will be transformed into an oasis of freedom and justice.

I have a dream that my four little children will one day live in a nation where they will not be judged by the colour of their skin but by the content of their character.

I have a dream today."

Martin Luther King envisioned a future where racial prejudice no longer existed, a future where the children of slaves could break bread with the children of slave owners. He invoked the spirit of the American dream, that all men are created equal, to shame governments and racists alike, saying that "one day this nation will rise up and live out the true meaning of this creed."

It is one of the greatest tragedies of all time that this great visionary did not live to see the first black President in the White House.

Martin Luther King paid the ultimate price for daring to dream. On April 4th, 1968 he was assassinated in Memphis, Tennessee, three and a half years after receiving the Nobel Peace Prize for combating racial inequality through non-violence.

The essence of Martin Luther King's vision for racial equality and an end to discrimination is crystal clear. The speech he made to define his vision was 17 minutes long, maybe two and a half thousand words.

Henry Ford, founder of the Ford Motor Company and inventor of the Model-T Ford, also had a vision. In its own way, Henry Ford's vision was equally remarkable, yet it was only three words long: democratise the automobile.

These three words have become one of the most famous corporate visions of all time. But what do they mean? What is the implication of those three words?

Before Henry Ford launched the Model-T, only small numbers of automobiles were being manufactured in America. In the late 19th and early 20th centuries, most cars were hand-made in Europe, playthings of the very wealthy. Manufacturers talked in terms of hundreds, rather than thousands, of unit sales. The majority of people in America were reliant on restrictive modes of transport. Buses and trains were the most popular form of getting about, and horse-drawn carts and shanks' pony were still the cheapest.

The fact of the matter was, the average American, unlike some of their wealthier neighbours, did not have the same comparative freedom of going where they pleased, when they pleased, or as often as they pleased. In other words, they lived in an undemocratic society where the privileged enjoyed benefits their less well-off neighbours could not.

In order to achieve his vision and to democratise the automobile, Ford was faced with the prospect of bringing the price of the motor car within reach of the average citizen. In so doing, as an entrepreneur, he acknowledged that one of the more risky aspects of his vision would be the real likelihood that he would turn away investors looking for a quick return on their money

By all accounts, Ford was a brilliant inventor, but, as history shows, he didn't invent the automobile, or the most visible example of the strategy he employed, the assembly line. What he did, brilliantly, was apply his knowledge and skills, and the knowledge and skills of his team, to facilitate the achievement of his vision.

In the winter of 1906, Henry Ford set up a secret plant in Detroit, where he and a number of trusted colleagues worked out how they were going to cut the cost of manufacturing motor cars. They made discovery after discovery, created innovation upon innovation. No challenge was too great. Discovering that the French were using specially developed alloys in their vehicles, he engaged a metallurgist and built his own steel mill to produce vanadium steel, a significantly lighter alloy than anything used in American production up to that time. This part of the journey took more than two years, but the car that finally emerged from the secret design section of his manufacturing plant weighed only 1200lbs, was powered by a twenty horsepower engine, was relatively easy to drive thanks to a two-speed, foot-controlled planetary transmission, and was already significantly cheaper to produce than its competitors.

The next step was to introduce factory automation. He applied the maxim: Everything can always be done better than it is being done. He and his team examined every aspect of assembly, and tested new methods to increase productivity. On a trip to Chicago, Ford inspected the way butchers at the stockyards used an overhead trolley when dressing beef. Each carcass was loaded onto the trolley, and as each one passed a line of butchers, a designated butcher removed a certain cut. This process continued down the line until nothing was left. By reversing the process, Ford and his team created the first automobile assembly line, dropping the assembly time for a Model T from twelve hours and thirty minutes, to five hours and fifty minutes.

By 1910, his goal to achieve savings through automation had made significant headway. In its first year of production, over 10,000 Model Ts were sold. The asking price of US$825 was still significantly higher than the prevailing average annual wage in the United States, but it was more affordable than any competitor vehicle. By this stage, Ford knew he could achieve his vision, but it would not come without a fight.

Over the next six years, Henry Ford fought his battle to democratise the automobile on two fronts. On one, he continued to look for opportunities to push the price of the Model T down. It was a time-consuming and complex process. On the other, he was waging a public relations campaign to keep his investors from pulling their funding out. In his favour was the fact that he had already anticipated the risk.

By 1912, the price of the Model T had been reduced to just under the average annual wage, at US$575. Two years later, by sacrificing profit margins even further, Ford managed to reduce the price to a staggering US$99, but his investors were almost at the end of their tether, just when Ford's plan kicked in.

As margins fell, sales exploded. In 1913, 248,000 Model Ts were sold in the US. Just as Ford had predicted, this figure increased exponentially each year. As sales increased through lower prices, profits soared. Net income rose from US$3 million in 1909 to US$25 million in 1914. In the same period, market share rocketed from 9.4% to a massive 48%. By 1920, Ford was selling one million Model T Fords p.a., and Henry Ford was one of the wealthiest men in America. And his investors were beaming.

The commitment and dedication that Ford and his team brought to achieving his vision may have been exhausting, but the end result, from every possible perspective, was well worth the effort. Ford changed the way the automobile world did things. Automation was locked into all future manufacturing processes, and, for the foreseeable future, the transportation needs of the average American were well and truly democratised.

Ford's legacy will never be forgotten. The foundation of that legacy, the vision on which he built a massive fortune, his vision to democratise the automobile, forever changed the shape of the automobile world.

I can almost hear you say, "How can I compare my vision with that of Henry Ford's? How can I achieve that level of success?"

However, that's not the point. What Ford did was to create an amazingly simple and pure vision that underpinned all the decisions that had to be made, and all the strategies that had to be implemented to achieve the required outcome. It's not the level of success we're dealing with here, but the genesis of it.

The point of telling Ford's story is to underpin the pure simplicity of a clear vision. Bill Gates is another you may not be comfortable comparing yourself to, but the vision he and Paul Allen articulated is in the same category of breathtaking simplicity as that envisioned by Henry Ford, one that also demonstrates that no two visions will ever be the same, not just in what they say, but how they say it.

Bill Gates is respected as one of the world's great entrepreneurs. There may be some who are reluctant to put him up on a pedestal as a great visionary, yet in many ways he deserves the accolade more than most. In an interview he gave after stepping down as head of Microsoft he recalled the vision which drove his incredible success.

"When Paul Allen and I started Microsoft over 30 years ago we had big dreams about software. We had dreams about the impact it could have. We talked about a computer on every desk and in every home. It's been amazing to see so much of that dream become a reality and touch so many lives. I never imagined what an incredible and important company would spring from those original ideas."

Notwithstanding the enormous talent Gates had as a computer programmer, in our minds there can be no doubting that it was Gates' preparedness to dream that set the company he and Allen founded on the path to becoming a multinational, multibillion dollar success.

Just for a moment imagine you are reading this book, not in the 21st century, with a clean, uncluttered desk in front of you, where a laptop is the only thing that spoils the vastness of your fake beech desktop. Instead, you have been transported back to a time when typewriters and telex machines were considered by most organisations as efficient communication technology, back to a time when computers were the advantage of very wealthy companies or filled the basements of government departments, a time when secretaries were employed to type, and paper clips were the irritating playthings of executives obsessed with the newest piece of electronic gadgetry – a calculator.

Its 1975, Bill Gates is just about to announce to his parents that he is leaving university to start his own company. He is very persuasive, and his parents relent, wishing him success. Since his early teens, Gates has been besotted by computers and computer programming. At school he wrote a program, which the administrators used to schedule classes; contrary to the image many have of Gates he used the program to ensure he was always slotted into classes with more girls than boys.

The catalyst that sparks Gates' decision to drop out of Harvard is the release of the Altair 8080 by MITS (Micro Instrumentation &Telemetry Systems), the machine that became synonymous with starting the microcomputer revolution. In partnership with his close friend, Paul Allen, Gates plans to be at the very heart of that revolution.

Together they hatch an audacious plot to convince MITS that they already have a working BASIC interpreter for the new computer. Bill Gates rings MITS and is caught unprepared when the company agrees to let them make a presentation. Small snag: not only don't they have a working interpreter, they don't even have an Altair 8080. Nevertheless, Gates agrees to a date for the presentation, and while Allen develops a simulator of the 8080, Gates develops the interpreter. When the day arrives for their presentation, they're ready, and although the interpreter has never been tested on a real Altair 8080, it passes with flying colours. The two entrepreneurs are rewarded with an agreement from MITS to market and distribute their interpreter as the Altair BASIC. A month later they register Microsoft.

The pair was off and running and most readers probably know the story from there.

The big breakthrough for Gates and Allen came five years later when IBM approached them with a request to produce a BASIC interpreter for its IBM PC. The relationship snowballed and the pair soon found themselves developing an operating system that would enable Microsoft to dominate the desktop computing space.

Initially, the dominant partner was IBM, but, gradually, it evolved, until Microsoft was an even bigger name, with a virtual monopoly of operating systems.

Back in 1975, Gates and Allen could have known none of this. Yes, they had every reason to believe that computers would be one of the most powerful tools of the future, but in what direction, in what form? Any doubts about their ability to envision a future place should be dispelled. They demonstrated an enormous capacity and ability as visionaries. They also demonstrated that they understood what would drive their vision. The clue, perhaps, is in the interview we referred to earlier when he stepped down as CEO of Microsoft.

Gates referred to the "big dreams they had about software" and the massive impact it could have on computing. But, when it came to articulating a vision for the future, he referred to computers, not software. By deliberately focusing their vision on a future place where there was a computer on every desk and in every home, Gates and Allen were acknowledging that their world existed within the broader context of computers, and everything that that world represented, to their customers. Without computer hardware, computer programming is irrelevant. Without computer programming, computer hardware is irrelevant. Of course, consumers don't always see it that way. When your average human being sits down in front of their laptop or PC and switches the machine on they expect it to come to life, with a screen full of icons that they can click on, and immediately be transported to the place they need to be.

Gates and Allen understood that the future would not be about computer nerds, but about everyday people. A future place where there would be a computer on every desk and in every home required it. In the early days, only astute consumers understood the intricacies of the operating system that ran their computer. The rest of us relied on computer experts to stay in touch and to understand what was happening as the computer revolution unfolded. In the end, most of us came to terms with the fundamentals of how computers operated, to the point where we could differentiate the purpose of Windows 7, or what INTEL meant, and how it all interfaced with the keyboard and monitor in front of us. But ask us to write a program, or understand how DOS works and we're lost. Our comfort in front of a computer today is very much the result of operating systems that we don't have to understand!

If you don't believe me, consider this statistic. Microsoft Windows was launched in 1985; today it is used on 90% of the world's 1 billion computers.

I can almost hear your mind ticking over: Gates, Allen, Henry Ford, even Martin Luther King, they were amazing people, great visionaries, people in a league of their own. Of course they were, and are, amazing people. But what was it, exactly, that set them apart. They weren't necessarily people with a higher IQ than you or me. They didn't necessarily come from better backgrounds, or receive, somehow, a different upbringing than most of us.

We believe the fundamental difference these great visionaries share is their capacity to envision what they can do better, or differently, the ability to clearly see a future place, distinctly and unequivocally. Can you achieve that same clarity of purpose, and overcome nagging doubts that these people are different?

If you want to judge visions by the company they keep, then Phillip Di Bella is in great company. The vision Phillip could see very clearly when he started Di Bella Coffee was built around an equally simple proposition as that used by Gates and, before him, Henry Ford.

As we have already pointed out, no two visions will ever be articulated in the same way. Gates was different to Ford; Di Bella will be different to either of them. What doesn't change is their capacity to envision a future place, and through articulating that vision, create clarity around the road map to get there.

Phillip defines the essence of his vision with three words that speak volumes, three words which provided him with all the signs required to get on the right track. Phillip's vision is a future place where customers engage with, and enjoy, the ultimate coffee experience.

"Every cup of coffee has a story. The ultimate coffee experience is the story I wanted Di Bella Coffee to provide. To deliver on that story requires an understanding of the importance of each part and a preparedness to constantly improve both our knowledge and the outcomes of that knowledge.

Consider the barista who makes your coffee. For the ultimate coffee experience, the barista must employ techniques and knowledge learnt and refined over time. They will have sourced their coffee from roasters who have combined science with their skill to blend and roast beans from around the world for optimum flavour.

The green beans used by the roasters have been on a journey of their own through cultivation, harvest and processing to capture the flavours unique to the earth of their specific region."

When you take each part of that story and break it down you not only begin to see what is behind Phillip's vision of the future, you also begin to see how it is possible to be accountable to a vision, and how the vision shapes the strategies for you to succeed.

To define it further, Phillip uses the mantra crop to cup to explain the level of control and the necessary choices he believes essential to delivering the ultimate customer experience.

"Crop to Cup is exactly what it suggests – an intimate knowledge of, and participation in, each of the steps that will ensure Di Bella Coffee is able to deliver on the customer's experience. It is a strategy that is painstakingly constructed to ensure each part is implemented. It accepts that the risk of omitting a single part has the potential to make the entire vision worthless."

When Phillip Di Bella outlines his vision it is obvious that not only was he comfortable with the idea of creating a vision, but he was also very comfortable with the process from the very outset. But not everyone is. Phillip acknowledges that many of the successful entrepreneurs he has met and engaged with didn't always set out with clarity around their vision. They had to work at it. In that regard, is Phillip blessed? Depends on what you regard as blessed. Not everyone in this world has the same sets of skills, but there is no reason why anyone with the desire to succeed cannot understand how to shape their vision of what could be.

Throughout this book we will explore Phillip Di Bella's vision, and the implication of his vision, in detail. We will identify the inhibitors and the motivators to creating a powerful vision. We will also explore the strategies Phillip needed to implement to deliver on his vision, and the way those strategies deliver on the values expected by the customer. For Henry Ford to democratise the automobile he needed to find a way to reduce the price of the motor car so that the ordinary family could afford it. He wanted the middle class of America to be able to enjoy the convenience and freedom the motor car represented, which, up until then, had been enjoyed exclusively by the wealthy. To reduce the price of the motor car meant he had to find ways to reduce the cost of production. It was that simple, or that hard, depending on whether you are a glass half-full or a glass half-empty kind of person.

There was also a financial imperative to Henry Ford's vision: he had to provide shareholders with a return that would keep them happy. He never lacked confidence in the ability of his vision to deliver on that outcome because his vision acknowledged what all astute marketers know: fulfil a customer need and they will come; deliver it at the right price point and they will come in huge numbers. When his shareholder's threatened to walk, Ford held firm. He cajoled and persuaded them to do the same. Fortunately for car lovers, most did. If we could have been a fly on the wall at one of those meetings I'm guessing that Henry Ford would have had the numbers prepared – an extrapolation of the profits driven by volume against the profits driven by margin. For Ford, the winner had to be volume, and that's how it worked out. Ford didn't gamble on the numbers, he simply read the market better than his competitors. The vision he had of that 'future place' was one where he had confidence the customer would want to be.

We doubt that Gates and Allen planned to measure their vision against financial returns, at least not in the days before Microsoft went public, in 1986. Both men were total and irrepressible computer nerds, and to envision a computer on every desk was the ultimate playground for them. The fact that it would be the pathway to unparalleled wealth is both a reflection on how well they envisaged their future place and how focused they were in following through on the strategies. Ultimately, those strategies delivered a 90% market share, driven in large part by the intuitive understanding Gates and Allen had that if they fulfilled a customer need, the customers would come.

Phillip Di Bella's vision is a future where customers engage with, and enjoy, the ultimate coffee experience. The price of coffee purchased at most cafes or restaurants is reasonably consistent. This is not a purchase made on a price, but on taste, quality and consistency. Customers will argue about which of those factors sit at the top of their priorities, but price will not be one of them. The key to Phillip's vision was that he knows his market; he spent months analysing his customers and what they valued most. His intelligence-gathering at the Farmers' Markets gave him one very clear message: people who enjoyed good coffee were discerning people who trusted their own judgement. These people would return, but only if their judgement was confirmed. Phillip knew he could win their loyalty, and he had a clear strategy of how he could do that.

Phillip, like Ford, like Gates and Allen, had a plan. The very soul of that plan was a vision of what could be. To create a vision takes imagination. It also takes a great deal of courage to conceptualise a different future and to have the wherewithal to chart a strategy to make it happen. Ford, Gates and Allen had the courage. Phillip Di Bella certainly had the courage to commit to his vision of that future place. How about you?

# 3

# Dare to Dream

In the first chapter, we pondered why so few people starting up companies failed to establish a vision as the foundation of their future. The research, both hard data and anecdotal, confirms that less than one-third of start-ups are founded on a vision.

In the second chapter, we examined some truly amazing visions and some truly amazing people, but we also asked what set these people apart? Or is that the wrong question? Should the question be: why don't we have the courage, or the confidence, to create a vision, and then allow that vision to unfold?

In this chapter we want you to ask yourself: do you have the courage to envision a future place? Do you have the same confidence Phillip Di Bella demonstrated when he first envisioned the ultimate coffee experience? If the answer is no, then ask yourself, why not? Is it because you don't know where to start? Is it because you feel uncomfortable with the idea? That it is somehow silly, or even stupid? Or perhaps you're still not convinced of the power of envisioning that future place. We suspect the answer partly lies in all of the above, but we suspect the underlying reason is fear of the process and what it may unleash.

I shared a story with Phillip when we began discussing this book, about the first time I engaged with a company vision. It was in the mid-eighties. I was CEO of the Brisbane arm of a national advertising agency and the senior management team had been invited to take part in a visioning process. For me it was enlightening, others were sceptical when the facilitator explained what was proposed. Most in the room were derisive of what they believed was a new form of water torture devised by the chairman. Looking back, Phillip and I both agree that what the executive team really needed, and what every entrepreneur needs before they even start, is to feel comfortable with the idea of creating a vision.

Fortunately, the facilitator knew what he was doing and invited everyone to vent their concerns and doubts. Slowly at first, but with ever increasing energy and engagement, they began to embrace the opportunity to step outside the shackles of fiscal policy or recruitment difficulties and to visualise what the company could become. By lunchtime, the mood in the room had changed significantly, and so had the body language. The folded arms were gone, the people in the room were more animated, and the ideas that flowed back and forth were creative – some perhaps too creative, but, once started, a wise facilitator will choose his moment carefully to rein that enthusiasm in.

We also need to be cautious about how and what we define as our vision. Martin Luther King described his vision as a dream. The phrase "I have a dream ..." has become a mantra for many. In a sense, the executive team I was part of was being given an opportunity to dream of a future that they wanted to be part of. But the term 'dream' is not one that sits comfortably with a lot of people. Phillip Di Bella is one of them. He sees it as a soft word, with the potential to be abused, particularly when a dream is the consequence of a dreamer.

"Is Richard Branson visionary?" Phillip asks rhetorically. "Of course he is. But Branson would brush aside suggestions of being a dreamer, because the mantle of dreamer doesn't fit comfortably with the image of a man whose personal mantra is Screw it, Let's do it. But there's no question in my mind that to most people Branson would be seen as visionary, with a powerful capacity to dream."

Some may argue the distinction of a visionary with a powerful capacity to dream is too subtle. We don't. In fact one of the fundamental distinctions between visionaries and dreamers is the capacity to put into action their dream. Before Martin Luther King's assassination he was credited with doing more to break down the prejudices of white Americans and alleviating the opposing fears of black Americans than any other individual in history. Gates and Allen didn't dream of a computer on every desk and then sit on their hands. Ford didn't call for the democratisation of the automobile and then stand by while others did the work.

The distinction between dreaming and visioning is not always crystal clear. A passion Phillip shares with Branson is the environment. Look hard at the environment movement and decide whether you see true visionaries or a large number of very passionate advocates with a dream. It's somewhat paradoxical: most of us would expect environmentalists to distinguish themselves as visionaries, yet very few can actually claim this title.

Ask yourself this question: do the leaders of the environment movements hold a clearly articulated vision of a future place or do they simply engage our fears? Two decades ago one of their own challenged environmentalists across the globe with that very same question: Does the environmental movement have the ability to create a vision, to articulate a future place that the members of the movement, and the world, would want to be a part of?

In 1994 an Adjunct Professor in the Environmental Studies Program at Dartmouth College, Hanover, USA, presented a paper to the Third Biennial Meeting of the International Society for Ecological Economics titled *Envisioning a sustainable world*.

The professor's name was Donella Meadows, and she opened her presentation by accusing leading environmentalists and humanitarians of failing in their duty to create a vision that would have the power to change the world. She went further, claiming the very capacity to be visionary was missing from the entire culture of the environment movement.

It was a startling accusation and a valuable insight into the struggle most people have in dreaming about what could be. Effectively, Meadows was accusing everyone responsible for the policy debate on the environment as being as lost as Alice in Wonderland!

When she addressed the meeting, Meadows was blunt:

"We talk about our fears, frustrations and doubts endlessly, but we talk only rarely and with embarrassment about our dreams. Environmentalists have been especially ineffective in creating any shared vision of the world they are working toward – a sustainable world in which people live within nature in a way that meets human needs while not degrading natural systems. Hardly anyone can imagine that world, especially not as a world they would like to live in."

It's a harsh criticism, but true. Very few of us give ourselves the authority to dream, and, as Meadows reaffirms, "building a responsible vision of a sustainable world is not a rational one. It comes from values, not logic," or right brain thinking, versus left. Instead of seeing the potential of an environmentally sustainable world, most of us associate environmentalism with logic steeped in a plethora of restrictions, prohibitions, regulations and, at the very core, sacrifices – think: climate change; think: clean energy; think: how much will it cost?

The most widely shared picture of a sustainable world is one of tight, centralised control with a low material standard of living, and not much fun. Instead of a vision, the future of the environment is seen in targets set by scientists to save the world from extinction.

Who in their right minds wants to be a part of a vision like that?

When Professor Meadows asked the world's top nutritionists, agronomists, economists, demographers and ecologists to create a vision for the future based on values, they were unable to do so.

The very people devoting their lives to ending world hunger were, at best, cynical about the value of visions and, at worst, were not even prepared to countenance such fantasies. Many rejected her question as fanciful, declaring that visions don't change anything. In fact, they chorused, you need to be careful with visions; they can be dangerous. Hitler, they said, had a vision, so how could you possibly trust visionaries.

Meadows became even more depressed when one of the highly respected environmentalists tentatively observed: "I have a vision, but it would make me feel childish and vulnerable to say it out loud."

In her paper, Professor Meadows' vision defined the problems confronted by the world today as rooted in hunger and driven by poverty. Look to the trouble spots throughout the world and without exception you will encounter both, places where respect for life is conditional on survival. Her solution, and the very essence of the vision she articulated was, "that every child born into the world is wanted, treasured and lovingly cared for."

It is impossible to miss the principle driver of Meadows' vision: a mother's love for her child. Even in a famine riddled country a mother's love is beyond doubt and can be seen in every wretched photograph ever taken of their mutual despair. But a mother's love can't ensure that a child will survive when there is no nourishment, and even less hope.

It would be too simplistic, and too convenient to suggest the resolution of Meadows' vision was to transfer food from the wealthy to buttress the poor. That leaves far too many potentially unanswered questions, including the resolution of corruption across the globe. Nor would a resolution invoking chemical intensive agriculture or the centralised control of food distribution be workable solutions, for the simple fact that they would invoke the rule of cause and effect. Increased chemical usage might create more cropping, but it would also require significant management of the residual effect of the chemicals. Centralised food distribution would challenge the very borders of democratic and non-democratic countries alike. These kinds of solutions would be no better than the negativity which had hamstrung the capacity of environmentalists to dream in the first place.

A vision where every child born into the world is wanted, treasured and is lovingly cared for demands that "fewer children are born and not one of them is wasted, that every child is born into the world wanted, treasured and lovingly cared for."

In expanding her vision, Professor Meadows began to articulate the changes her vision could achieve, and how. "Every person," she said, "can become all that she or he is capable of becoming, in a world ... where cultures are diverse and tolerant, where information flows freely, untainted by cynicism. In my vision, food is raised and prepared as consciously and lovingly as are children, with profound respect for nature's contribution, as well as that of people."

Professor Meadows' vision is compelling. She was also a realist, and acknowledged that there would be many who would be uncomfortable in the presence of such visionary language. But Meadows persisted because she understood that there is a place inside every one of us, despite the protests we may make, that desperately wants a world something like the one she described, and that our visions, when we are willing to admit them, are astonishingly alike.

Phillip Di Bella enthuses about the power of such a vision in a commercial context.

We are sitting in his office. He spins the monitor of his computer so that we can both see the screen. He's googled the Virgin website and points to Virgin's vision statement.

"This is Branson's vision for Virgin's contribution to a sustainable lifestyle. There are striking similarities between this ...," Phillip points at the screen, "... and the vision that Professor Meadows and her team of reluctant environmentalists finally articulated to end hunger in the world."

Phillip has recently returned from a short stay at Necker Island, Richard Branson's island in the Caribbean. The two men talked at some length about what each sees as the necessary attributes of successful entrepreneurs. Phillip, who has just received a Corporate Citizen Award from the Brisbane Lord Mayor, says he is inspired by Branson, but that Branson is not his inspiration. Nor does he agree with all of Branson's philosophies or mantras, but is impressed with the way Virgin manage their corporate responsibilities in regards to such critical factors as the environment. Phillip continues:

> "A key reason behind the success of Richard Branson is his belief in the power of entrepreneurship and innovation. He does not shy away from the business of making money, but understands that Virgin has a corporate responsibility to provide leadership for a sustainable lifestyle.
>
> Virgin's vision goes to the very heart of the dilemma by acknowledging that the principle of cause and effect is nowhere more evident than in the impact our lifestyles have on each other, and on the planet."

On their website, Virgin points to this as a key plank in making more responsible choices about how they should do business, drawing unintended but intriguing similarities between the vision of Professor Meadows and that espoused by Virgin. In part, the Virgin Vision reads:

> So far, a sustainable lifestyle has been associated with sacrifice or compromise, giving up the choice and freedom we currently enjoy. Virgin's vision is the opposite of this. We believe that living sustainably doesn't have to mean cutting back or frugality, and responsibility shouldn't be dull or difficult.

Our vision is to contribute to creating happy and fulfilling lives which are also sustainable – surely a vision worth aspiring to?

The road map that Virgin gives to its thousands of employees is as succinct as the vision it wants to achieve:

We want our Virgin companies to provide responsibly produced, sustainable, low carbon services and products that are desirable, easy to use and good value above all else so that our customers can enjoy their lifestyles safe in the knowledge that Virgin is acting responsibly on their behalf.

The road map describes a need for the company to embrace minimal emissions of carbon and greenhouse gases, to ensure responsible use of the planet's finite resources, while working towards the alleviation of poverty and the fair treatment of individuals. But it is the last couple of lines of the Vision statement that capture Phillip Di Bella's imagination.

He points at the monitor and laughs. "You can almost hear Branson saying the last couple of lines, they are so typically Branson." Phillip reads them out loud. "'Show that change isn't dull or involving sacrifice – think of what we gain not what we give up.'"

To many, John Lennon was the face of a generation that dared, not just to dream, but to challenge the essential fabric of a conservative society shaped by the bloody outcomes of two world wars. As one of the four Beatles, and flanked by an army of rock groups, musicians and performers, Lennon helped fuel a generation's desire to be free and unshackled by outdated mores and conservative thinking; a generation which believed it had the right to dream.

I remember the first time I heard Lennon's song *Imagine*. I was in London, packing to return to Australia. The ideas it evoked, of no countries or borders or religions to define people so that the world would be united, were incredibly powerful. The fact that I was just about to board a plane that would take me across many of the trouble spots in the world made the lyrics especially poignant.

*Imagine* is one of the most played songs of all time. It is ranked number 3 on *Rolling Stone*'s 500 all-time greatest songs list. In an interview with *Rolling Stone*, Yoko Ono, Lennon's widow, declared, "*Imagine* was just what John believed: that we were all one country, one world, one people."

*Rolling Stone* summed up the essence of the song when they described it as "… an enduring hymn of solace and promise that has carried us through extreme grief, from the shock of Lennon's death in 1980 to the unspeakable horror of September 11th. It is now impossible to imagine a world without *Imagine*."

I have no doubt that, had he lived, John Lennon would have continued to fight for what he saw as a future place worth fighting for, a place without greed or hunger or disunity. Until he was gunned down outside the Dakota building in New York he had actively sought ways to bring his dream to fruition. He was not a fool. When he lamented that people may think of him as a dreamer, he was actually articulating the negative connotation that so many attach to the word, and to the idea of dreaming. What that lament does is capture the essential difference between dreaming and visioning.

Lennon tried to encapsulate the heart and soul of a generation in a song, and he almost pulled it off. He appealed to his generation to join a crusade to unite the world. Nowadays, though, I wonder how many baby boomers joined that fight so the world could be as one. Perhaps, what began for millions in a generation as a grand ambition to realise a dream somehow lost its way and became caught up in the day-to-day reality of careers and the mortgage belt.

To dream is not to be vulnerable, as so many people seem to think. To dream of a future place is not a sign of weakness. But to fail to fulfil that dream is at the heart of the differential between dreaming and visioning. The single most defining factor that differentiates dreamers from visionaries is that dreamer's dream and visionaries make it happen.

Phillip Di Bella's advice is simple: give yourself the authority to see the future. Become like those who have recognised the power of a vision and have transformed that vision into success. Use those people as your guide, as your mentor, and ignore the pessimists, the faint-hearted, the cynics and the dreamers.

# 4

# The power of your imagination

The concept of left brain-right brain is one that most people are familiar with. The idea evolved out of research conducted by an American psycho-biologist named Roger Sperry, who concluded that the human brain has two different ways of thinking. One way, Sperry contended, used the right part of the brain to think visually, by processing information in an intuitive and simultaneous way. In essence, the right brain looks at the whole picture rather than the details that make up the picture.

The other way, using the left brain, Sperry concluded, thinks verbally and processes information analytically and sequentially by first looking at the pieces and then putting them together in a structured way to create the whole picture. Sperry won a Noble Prize for his work in 1981, although, subsequently, there have been studies that show the brain is not divided as literally as he suggested. But nobody has been prepared to completely discount the left brain-right brain principle, and the concept still carries a great deal of respect.

The theory of left brain-right brain works like this. People who are right brain dominant are more suited to expressive and creative tasks. The strengths of right brain people is in recognising faces, expressing and reading emotions, they tend to be musically inclined, have a good appreciation of colour and the use of colour, have strong intuition and high levels of creativity. It would be hard not to believe that John Lennon was anything but right brain dominant, or that Martin Luther King would not have been a person with a strong leaning to the right.

People who are left brain dominant would be considered more adept at tasks that involve logic, language and analytical thinking. The strengths of left brain people are seen as good language skills, sound logical thinking with a capacity for critical thinking, numbers and reasoning. There is a tendency to identify left brain dominance with professions such as scientist or engineers, or even astronauts.

Talk to Phillip Di Bella and the immediate impression you gain is of a right brain dominant personality. I haven't asked, but I doubt Phillip's ambitions as a youngster included astronaut. However, talk to Phillip for any length of time and the conversation will cover a broad range of interests and ideas. One minute he could be discussing the passion he has for education, the next he's guiding an employee on the details of a complex blend for roasting. This is when left brain-right brain theorists start to waver; the idea that a person is either entirely left brain dominant or right brain dominant loses credibility when someone can't be pigeonholed into one or the other.

Caught up in this debate is the belief that somehow right brain dominance is necessary to envision the future, or that right brain dominant people are better at envisioning a better place. The truth, of course, is not that polarised. In the advertising business, I worked with a great number of people who were considered creative geniuses. What I always found was that the really good creative people, or right brain dominant according to the theory, were also very logical and good critical thinkers.

Equally it is too simplistic to suggest that engineers or scientists are not also creative thinkers.

I once took a test to analyse my own left brain-right brain dominance and was surprised to find the result was scored 9 left brain to 11 right brain. I was almost on the cusp, equal parts left, equal parts right. And, frankly, I suspect that most people would achieve similar results.

Phillip Di Bella understands the premise behind right brain-left brain, but says he has never taken a test to find out.

"I don't necessarily hold with the left brain- right brain theory," Phillip tells me on one occasion, "but I definitely accept that some people may feel uncomfortable envisioning their future, particularly people who have been raised or trained to analyse everything to death. Scientists and engineers must be sceptical; they are trained to remove any thought that could be considered irrational or subjective".

"What I do acknowledge is that under the auspices of the left brain-right brain premise, envisioning is a right brain activity and that the ability to see the place where you want to be will not necessarily come from rational analysis. My ability to envision the future is more about my emotional connection with my hopes and ambitions, than it is about trying to rationalise what could be possible."

This is not an uncommon response to the left brain-right brain premise. Ask any successful entrepreneur and we would be surprised if they didn't categorically reject the idea that the capacity to envision or dream comes from rational analysis. Their preparedness to think outside the box and to use their imagination is at the heart of every entrepreneur's success.

Yet something seems to hold people back from using their imaginations.

Convention and timidity are part of it. Most of us have a natural aversion to being out of step with others. It is a by-product of people's insecurity. So we conform, and we accept what we see around us as normal, and we "fit in". When we make decisions, we do so not just on the basis of what "we" think, but what others think as well. To conform is a major influence in our lives, and the more insecure we are, the more likely we are to be influenced by what others think. It isn't easy to break out from these constraints – and yet we do, frequently, without even realising it.

In fact, when was the last time you went to the movies?

Lee Child's Jack Reacher novels have a legion of fans. Reacher is described as a mountain of a man, six feet five inches tall, heavily built with a thick neck and hands the size of dinner plates. The novels have been an outstanding success, with a massive following, male and female. Now Jack Reacher has been brought to life in the movies. Intriguingly the male actor who plays this larger than life hero is 11 inches – one inch shy of a foot – shorter than the fictional Reacher, and although extremely fit and physical does not quite meet the description of the Jack Reacher who appears in every book.

Tom Cruise is a phenomenally successful actor. The *Mission Impossible* series cemented Cruise's place alongside other great action stars. He plays the roles with an assurance that defies any rational consideration of what may be considered physical restrictions. The mind plays tricks, not just because the director of a movie employs them, but because we want to believe.

Prior to the release of the first Jack Reacher movie, there was enormous speculation around the ability of Tom Cruise to pull off the role. The question asked was "is he Reacher enough?" Fans of the books flooded social media with criticisms of the producer's choice of lead actor. Twenty-four per cent of online mentions were negative, the highest percentage of negative numbers the research firm Fizziology had ever seen for a particular actor in an upcoming movie. Then the producers released a trailer, two months out from the movie release. The trailer was compelling; it showed Cruise in a number of sequences from the movie. The last shot saw him get out of a car in which he was being chased, let the handbrake go and, as the car starts to gather momentum, calmly walk to the busy footpath. By the time the car chasing our hero comes into view, Cruise has already taken his place in the watching crowd, appearing as tall as, if not taller than, the other men around him.

As the chase car closes on the slowing, but now empty, car, a glimmer of understanding flashes in the eyes of the man standing next to Cruise. He takes his cap off and offers it to Jack Reacher, who calmly pulls it on, just as the chase car roars past in pursuit of the runaway.

After the release of the trailer, research once again asked the question, is Cruise Reacher enough? Negative comments dropped from 24% to 13%.

I tell this story for a very simple reason. The movie world is the greatest proof of our ability to suspend disbelief and to allow our imagination to be free to believe what we want to believe. Walk outside after a matinee into bright sunshine and the right you gave yourself sitting in the cinema to suspend disbelief disappears in the blink of an eye. Outside, the world is normal, almost boring, perhaps there is also a sense of disappointment forming in your head that, out here, on the street, life is suddenly back to black and white reality.

The intriguing question is: why are we prepared to suspend disbelief in the cinema and allow our imaginations to take over, when, outside, we retreat back into our shell?

Look around. What do you see? People going about their business, signs outside shops promoting their wares, a bus trundling along the street with advertising on the side promoting one of the large banks, a young man escorting an elderly lady across the street, an older man showing courtesy by making room on the footpath for you to pass. As we said, everything back to normal, no daredevil stunts with cars crashing into buildings or armed men being chased down the street. What you see are people doing expected things in expected ways, or, in other words, people conforming to the expected.

Inside the cinema we watched Jack Reacher pull off stunts that we accepted unquestioningly. Outside, in the bright light of day, we would probably laugh, even cringe if someone was stupid enough to not conform.

So what has all this got to do with creating a vision?

Envisioning is about giving yourself permission to break with convention, to say no to conformity and to use your imagination. Envisioning is the power to use your imagination in such a way that you can jump over the perceived reasons why you shouldn't.

It's about accepting that the starting place for your vision may be an irrational place.

Ask yourself this simple question: is it possible to eradicate hunger in the world? Answer carefully; your response will give you a very good insight into whether you have given yourself permission to envision a future place or whether you still need to do so.

The rational, objective answer to the question is an overwhelming 'no'. Your rational mind argues that it is simply not possible to resolve all of the problems associated with hunger, to be able to make such a major commitment, or to deliver on such a massive undertaking.

If your answer was 'no', go to the front of the permission-given-here queue.

If your answer was 'yes', but you then allowed your rational mind to analyse and contemplate the question and then to reject it because of the obstacles in the way of reaching the desired outcome, then your answer is still effectively 'no' and you should join the same queue.

Phillip Di Bella's answer to the question is an unequivocal 'yes!' No buts, no maybes, no pragmatic rationalisation.

Professor Meadows' vision of eradicating hunger from the world is a heartfelt, soulful vision. Yes, it is a vision that is going to take a long time to accomplish because of the sheer scope and enormity of the task. For that reason alone the pragmatist in each of us would be on display, and it is how we deal with the pragmatic, the rational, that determines whether we have the capacity to envision, and to then to go on to apply that vision to achieving success as an entrepreneur.

If you are still sceptical about the power of envisioning, consider how many people there are in the world who believes in God. The figure is in the billions, right? Every one of those people believes in something they can't see. They trust because they have belief. That's what we're trying to open up here – the power to believe in what you can achieve and the power to use your imagination to see what you can achieve. Vision is not a rational process, even though it will be your rational sense that must inform, and, ultimately, it is your rational thought that will keep your vision focused. But it can't, and shouldn't, start there!

Imagine the power of your vision. What could you achieve if you gave yourself the authority to dream?

# 5

## Who cares what the customer needs?

Most entrepreneurs make mistakes on their journey. Phillip Di Bella openly admits where his judgement may have been off, or his people management skills needed fine tuning. Mistakes are inevitable. Branson writes frequently about the mistakes he made and the lessons he learnt as a result. In *Screw it, Let's do it* Branson writes:

"Some you win and some you lose. Be glad when you win. Don't have regrets when you lose. Never look back. You can't change the past. I try to learn from it. We can't all run big airlines or trains. Many people have more modest goals. But whatever your dream is, go for it."

One of the greatest ironies in life is that mistakes rarely happen if you don't have a dream to go for, or if you don't set yourself goals to reach. But there is a significant difference between goal setting (and achieving them), and setting a vision. Unfortunately, all too often the two are blurred by people who interchange goals with vision, without really understanding the difference.

Phillip Di Bella is passionate about setting goals. From a very young age he had a goal to be a millionaire by the time he turned 30. He achieved it at 28. He contends that a big part of his success began when he started setting goals, often small tasks that he wanted to achieve.

However, the difference between Phillip's vision of the ultimate coffee experience and his goal of becoming a millionaire by the age of 30 is like chalk and cheese.

In a book published more than 20 years ago titled *Built to Last: Successful Habits of Visionary Companies*, the authors, James Collins and Jerry Porras, coined the acronym BHAG, or big hairy audacious goal, to define goals that are more strategic and emotionally compelling than just standard, run-of-the-mill goals, like the ones we set in high school or the day-to-day goals we may use to guide our companies.

In defining visionary companies, Collins and Porras argued that these organisations use business goals to establish short-term, even medium-term outcomes, such as profit goals, workforce development goals and so forth. More audacious goals were longer-term, even 10 to 30 year goals, set to progress the company towards an envisioned future.

"A truly audacious goal," the authors claimed, "is clear and compelling, serves as a unifying focal point of effort, and acts as a clear catalyst for team spirit. It has a clear finish line, so the organisation can know when it has achieved the goal."

Go, Jim and Jerry!

We agree with your definition of goal, but we're not so sure about the premise behind your proposition – and we want to clear up any confusion there might be on what we consider a critical point for budding entrepreneurs.

A goal is not a vision, no matter how you dress it up, not even if the authors believed they were starting a new trend. Worse still, a clever acronym doesn't make the disguise any more acceptable. No matter how big, a goal of any nature will never be a vision. All the clever rhetoric does is create uncertainty. To be sure, goals are an integral part of planning, but they are a separate stage of planning than establishing a vision.

To understand the confusion perpetuated by the theory put forward by Collins and Porras, trawl the internet and you will find an endless stream of blogs, websites or media sites discussing BHAGS. Whether the authors of these sites are quoting directly from *Built to Last: Successful Habits of Visionary Companies* or simply identifying their own versions of BHAGs is irrelevant; either way, we believe they are perpetuating a level of confusion that is both unnecessary and unfortunate.

Some of the examples cited in these blogs in support of Jim and Jerry's proposition are claimed to belong to some of the most successful organisations on this planet and, according to the current commentary on the internet, each one is defined as a Big Hairy Audacious Goal.

AIESEC (Association Internationale des Etudiants en Sciences Economiques et Commerciales) defines itself on its web page as the world's largest student-run organisation, present in over 110 countries and territories and with over 80,000 members. The focus of AIESEC is on providing a platform for youth leadership development by offering young people the opportunity to be global citizens, to change the world, and to get experience and skills that matter today. According to several commentators, or bloggers, AIESEC's BHAG is: to engage and develop every young person in the world.

An amazing vision, most definitely, but a goal, even a big goal, we're not so sure.

Amazon.com, like the river, needs no introduction. In an amazingly short time, Amazon has, to all intents and purposes, become the largest purveyor of books in the world. Amazon's BHAG, as quoted on one blog, is eminently clear and concise: Every book, ever printed, in any language, all available in less than 60 seconds. Do we agree that this is a goal, no matter how big? We think not. To our thinking this is a very good example of a clearly stated vision. We actually don't have to go further than Amazon's own website to confirm their agreement.

On the Amazon website you will find an FAQ page. One of the frequently asked questions is: what is Amazon's vision? The answer is: to be the earth's most customer centric company; to build a place where people can come to find and discover anything they might want to buy online. Not exactly what was quoted by the blogger online, but heading in very much the same direction.

Or consider another computer giant, IBM. One blogger claimed the company's BHAG was to commit to a $5 billion gamble on the 360.

For those who don't remember this piece of ancient computer history, the 360 was a mainframe computer system introduced in the mid-60s. It was designed to cover the gamut of computer needs, from small to large, in both commercial and scientific arenas. By way of comparison, for those who understand these things, the System/360 models announced in 1964 ranged in speed from 0.0018 to 0.034 MIPS, a fraction of the computing speed that today's processors, such as Intel, offer the most basic lap-top user.

At the time, IBM's gamble was a massive leap forward for computing, but was their decision to commit to a $5 billion gamble on the 360 a goal or a vision? We're not sure that it qualifies as either; we would suggest it is most likely a high level strategy.

To be successful in life you need to understand the difference between a vision and goals. To be successful as an entrepreneur you MUST understand the difference. Not to understand will leave you in a very uncertain place, where confusion rather than clarity rules. Both a vision and goals are integral parts of the one plan, but they each play a different role. If you are unable to discern the difference, it is highly unlikely that you will go on to reach the pinnacles you are aiming for. Their different roles are also the reason why we are critical of the confusion created by referring to visions as goals, or, by attempting to create a new dynamic such as BHAG. But, we also believe that by understanding the difference, you begin to identify the potential power of your vision versus the very necessary, but very pragmatic, importance of setting goals.

The dictionary is a good starting point to understanding the difference between a vision and a goal, but it also leaves our question largely unresolved. The distinction begins with the use of language. Goals are defined through the use of concise words such as a target, or a purpose or objective, maybe even an ambition or a destination. These are all descriptors that have an outcome; they can be measured in terms of success. Kicking a goal in football is a measurable outcome; a goal to achieve a profit extraction ratio of 12% is equally measurable.

On the other hand, vision is described in the dictionary using softer, less definitive words, such as an image, an idea or a dream, nothing very tangible or decisive in any of those words. And if you think they are soft, what about hopes and ideals, even fantasy, daydream or flight of fancy. Certainly not words that you would expect to be able to be measured.

At least the dictionaries give us a distinction between the two words, but it is still a long way from clarifying the critical point of difference.

Perhaps we need to look at this in a different way.

We have already written about Bill Gates' and Paul Allen's vision: A computer on every desk and in every home. Google "BHAG" and it is almost inevitable that you will find their vision in an article extolling the virtues of setting Big Hairy Audacious Goals. When we did just that we also came across a BHAG for Hewlett-Packard, which stated that the company was striving to be one of the best managed corporations in the world.

Now ask yourself this question: which of these statements do you believe will best fulfil a customer need? To be one of the best managed corporations in the world or to work with a company who sees its future inextricably linked to there being a computer on every desk and in every home? Consider the two statements carefully. Both have completely different expectations, yet while both are laudable ambitions only one of them can fully satisfy a customer need.

Think about it. Do you see opportunity and power in the notion of a computer on every desk, or is there greater power in being one of the best managed corporations in the world?

In 1939, Dave Packard and Bill Hewlett tossed a coin in a small suburban garage in Palo Alto, California, to decide whose name would go first in the company they were planning to form. No prizes for guessing who lost the coin toss, or that the company in question went on to become one of the great computing companies in the world. Today, Hewlett-Packard is best described as a multinational information technology corporation. Their product line includes personal computing devices, servers, storage devices, networking products, software and a diverse range of printers and other imaging devices marketed to both households and small to medium sized businesses. HP also has a strong services and consulting business around its products and partner products.

Hewlett-Packard has been one of the great success stories of the computing revolution, but there are many who say that HP is on the decline, and that the cracks have been showing for some years.

In 2009 HP was the 9th largest brand in the world. By 2012 it was ranked at number 15 by Interbrand, an internationally recognised branding company that releases an annual ranking of the best global brands[2]. Compounding this fall, in 2012 Chinese based computing company Lenova became the world's largest PC manufacturer, taking over the mantle held for years by HP.

Interbrand's summary of HP's performance in the 2012 brand rankings focused on the turbulence experienced by the company over the preceding years, in particular the departure and appointment of three different CEOs since 2010. In their commentary, Interbrand also forecast HP's likely fall from the number one position as the world's largest PC manufacturer:

---

2　　To qualify, brands must have a presence on at least three major continents and have a broad geographic coverage in growing and emerging markets. Interbrand's criteria also states that 30% of revenues must come from outside the home country, and no more than 50% of revenue should come from one continent.

"The internal instability has resulted in the lack of a cohesive business strategy or brand strategy, which threatens both financial results and HP's reputation. HP has retreated from the mobile devices and tablets that make up more and more of end- consumers' technology purchases. Lenovo is predicted to hit the number one spot in the PC market, layering further pressure on the consumer."

In 2012 HP announced that the company was planning to lay off 27,000 employees after posting a 2nd quarter profit decline of 31%. This figure was later increased to more than 29,000 employees. Market analysts suggested at the time that the profit decline, and the need to lay off so many employees, was a direct result of the growing popularity of smart phones and tablets, products the company had resolved to remove from their product mix in the previous year.

To our way of thinking, this simple story about Hewlett-Packard clearly establishes the differential between the power of articulating a vision versus the pragmatism of setting goals.

A few paragraphs back we asked you to consider whether the BHAG articulated by Microsoft, or that purported to belong to Hewlett-Packard, better delivered on what we described as a customer need. It was not meant to be a trick question, because, frankly, there is only one answer: the real power lies with Gates' and Allen's vision of a computer on every desk and in every home

To achieve the vision that Gates and Allen established of *a computer on every desk, in every home* required them to establish a number of goals and set a range of strategies in place to achieve their goals. One of the most fundamental goals the pair would need to have set was to build all software so that it was accessible to anyone, regardless of their computer skills. Another goal would have been to make all their software compatible with every hardware manufacturer's equipment. Apple was the most significant challenge Microsoft needed to overcome in this regard, and that story is very well documented.

Gates and Allen may well have set themselves a goal to become one of the world's best managed corporations, just as they could have set themselves the goal to be one of the world's most customer focused organisations. Either goal could have proven to be essential to achieving their ultimate vision, but those goals, just like the goal to build compatible software did not, and could not, replace the core vision of the company.

Search the HP website as hard as we could, we found no reference to a company vision statement. We found a great deal about the company's struggle to stay relevant in the marketplace, which leads to the inevitable question: could it be that in HP's drive to become one of the best managed corporations in the world, that their business focus was less on their customer's needs and more on resolving the structural problems that had beset the company as it struggled to remain competitive? Was the company so consumed with the immediate need to shore up corporate management that it took its eyes off the changes that were occurring in the marketplace and, in that regard, to set goals accordingly?

There must be a reason why a company would move away from core products that were in growing demand in the marketplace, products such as mobile devices and tablets, products that have become such a key part of consumer lifestyles (and not just their computing needs). Did HP do so in response to a clearly stated vision of what the company's future place looked like? A vision which engaged with the customer's needs? Obviously we don't have the answer to that question, but there is no available evidence to suggest otherwise.

There is a tragic parallel to HP's fall that highlights the importance of customer need.

More than fifty years earlier, Theodore Levitt used the expression marketing myopia to define the mistake many companies made in focusing on the goods and services produced rather than on the needs the goods fulfilled. He used the example of the declining fortunes of the American railways to show how an organisation focusing on the wrong vision could come unstuck.

Levitt argued that the reason the railways were in decline was because they refused to see themselves in the transport business instead of in the railway business. He contended that they were going broke not because the need for moving people or freight had disappeared, but because the railways, by being so narrow in their vision of their future place, allowed other providers to fulfil the customer's need. Had the railways defined themselves as part of transport, they would have found a way to deliver freight from the railhead to the warehouse 20 miles away. Instead of finding a way to fulfil the need of the customer, they left the door open for other, smarter entrepreneurs to come up with a solution to the customer's need to have freight delivered to their door.

Perhaps the railways, like HP, were more focused on being the best managed organisation in the country rather than envisioning a future place where they "delivered customer focused transport solutions."

***

At the start of this chapter we debated the difference between establishing a vision and setting goals. We started the discussion by contending that the difference between Phillip Di Bella's goal of becoming a millionaire before the age of thirty, and his vision of the ultimate coffee experience was chalk and cheese. Yet they were intrinsically linked.

When someone envisions a future place, like Phillip did, they are not only setting a goal by which they will measure their success, they are also laying out the most important aspect of their strategic plan, the foundation on which they will build their empire. Phillip envisioned a future place where his customers would always enjoy the ultimate cup of coffee. That would be their reward for being loyal to the Di Bella brand. No questions, no doubts, no wavering on the part of his customers, because they trusted Phillip's commitment to his vision. But how could they? Most of them, if prompted, would be unlikely to be able to quote Phillip's vision; they may have heard it said, or read about it in promotional material, but nobody was ever going to say, "Look, here's Phillip Di Bella's vision, and it will change my mind about coffee."

That's because Phillip Di Bella's vision, like Gates' and Allen's, or Henry Ford's is not only about the customer's need, but it is everything about the customer that Phillip needs to understand to put his vision into action. When Phillip envisioned a place where the ultimate coffee experience would occur, time after time, after time, after time, after…, that place started to reveal what it would take to achieve his vision.

In the same way, Gates and Allen didn't define their future place by what, or whose, computers would be on every desk and in every home, because they didn't need to. Their vision was that the computers would be there and their operating system would have a home. When they established Microsoft in the mid-70s, they had no idea of the sheer scale or size their business would become, but by envisioning a computer on every desk, they identified the potential scope for operating systems. Their experience and knowledge told them that for computers to be on desks in every home the system would need to be user friendly – in fact it would need to work without relying on the operator being a computer nerd like them. This was the thinking that would drive their planning and their goals.

So, where is Gates' and Allen's vision today? There is a computer on virtually every desk and in every home in the developed world, and countries such as India and China and Indonesia, with huge middle-class populations, are following rapidly in those same footsteps. In 1975, Gates and Allen had no way of knowing that their system would be used in 90% of all those computers. Frankly, a

10% share of the market would have still made them billionaires.

Henry Ford's vision was not to build a smarter, more refined motor car. Ford envisioned a future place where almost everyone could afford a motor car, making the motor car an essential, unconditional part of every person's life. Today, almost every Australian family has at least one motor car in the garage, most have two, many have three or more.

# 6

# Vision begets goals

Some people refer to vision as an abstract concept, and perhaps it is. But defining it as abstract doesn't take anything away from its potential as a powerful concept.

Gates and Allen envisioned a computer on every desk and then developed a strategic plan to capitalise on that vision. When Ford determined the need to democratise the automobile he identified goals and then strategies, fully aware that there would be significant pain in them for his shareholders, but equally convinced that his strategy was right.

Strategic planning is much more than envisioning a future place. Phillip Di Bella set out the vision he wanted to achieve and then developed his plan to achieve it. Part of that plan was setting the goals he needed to achieve on the journey, and the strategies and actions he would have to implement to achieve them.

We doubt that there was ever an occasion when Bill Gates or Paul Allen, or Henry Ford, ever referred to their vision as a goal. Their capacity to understand the difference is reflected in the way they went about building their empires. To democratise the automobile Ford understood his strategy must be to reinvent the way automobiles were made, so that he could reduce the cost of production. His goal, therefore, not his vision, was to reduce the cost by half, and then by half again. The battle Ford had with his shareholders highlights this ongoing strategy; in fact the first part of his story is an investor's nightmare.

From the first time he and his development team emerged from their secret development plant, Henry Ford's focus was to find ways to reduce costs. The goals that drove this strategy had a target for completion. Invariably the actions and tactics he used to achieve his goals impacted on the bottom line. Even the most committed R&D exponent knows that you cannot invest in change without incurring significant expense. It may not be simply dollars that show up clearly in an expense column, but the investment in change may be more frequently shown in human resource expenditure (or sacrifice), which is not always captured as clearly as it should be in the same expense lines. As his costs grew, the history books show that Ford was forced to sit down with his investors on more than one occasion to persuade them to forgo their profit entirely, in order that he could achieve his target for that particular year. But this was not a shallow operator skimming the cream from the top to salt away into his bank accounts; Ford had a very clear plan, and a clear set of goals and strategies that he had every confidence in, and which he stuck to regardless, and which, in the end, paid off handsomely.

Setting goals has long been acknowledged as the way we achieve progress through life. At school it may be as simple as setting a target for a mark in an exam, or to achieve a specific sporting target, such as kicking a goal, or scoring runs. It could even be a performance target, anticipating that running five or ten kilometres a week will improve fitness, which, in turn, will improve performance. Personal goals expand as we move through our lives. We set goals for financial outcomes to protect our families and, if we are smart, establish goals that reflect the importance of our own self-being and the importance of participating in a loving and healthy family life.

Goal setting is one of the most rewarding aspects of our lifestyle. There is a bonus to setting goals, which we believe all too often goes unheralded. We lead busy lives and often don't reflect on what we have achieved. Achieving a goal is a significant milestone, but sometimes we become dispassionate about our achievements. The fact that we saved the money inside the deadline we set ourselves is a bonus. So is the early delivery of the motor car, but then we move on. What we may not rate highly enough is the sense of wellbeing our efforts bring to us.

A significant body of research has been undertaken looking at the link between achieving desired goals and the resultant subjective impact on our wellbeing. What the findings tell us is that the bigger the goal, and the more effective our strategy is to achieve the goal, the greater the sense of subjective wellbeing we experience.

Consider the most basic of goals – saving up for a specific purchase, or even saving for retirement. The goal might be articulated in a variety of different ways, but what will be consistent is the need for the goal to be measurable in terms of the amount you need to save and when you propose to have the money. So, the goal might be to save $20,000 to purchase a new car within two years. Nothing more really needs to be said. The goal is simple, the measures are clear, the next thing is to identify 'how'.

Of course the how may be as simple as putting aside a certain amount of money from each regular salary or wage payment. It may engage with a slightly more complex process of opening an interest bearing account to speed up the process. It may also involve a personal commitment to deposit any windfall amounts into the same deposit account, rather than use it to buy something else you crave.

Stepping up from personal goals to organisational goals is not complex, or difficult, although the transition is not always seen so transparently. Organisations are by their very nature self-centred, in much the way we as individuals are. Adapting to goals that are not about self becomes a key part of learning to become a team player, and for any commercial venture the immediate and primary goal is profitability. Prioritising goals, therefore, becomes a task about identifying what is best for the organisation and how best you, as part of the team, contribute to that success. Implicit in the setting of goals for any organisation is that you as the individual are acknowledged and cared for within the strategies that make the organisation successful.

The discipline of setting goals, then, engages another part of our makeup – managing the outcome of those goals. While we might often set goals subconsciously, without structured thought as to how we will achieve them, most of the goals we set are planned, as is the process of achieving them. The fact that it may be subconscious is really not relevant. What is relevant is that we actually go through a process.

Setting goals may sometimes appear to exist separately to your vision. Don't be fooled. When Phillip Di Bella set himself the goal to be a millionaire by the time he turned 30, that goal could only work if Phillip had a strategy to achieve it. In turn, the strategy could only exist if he had an overarching vision that kept him motivated towards the outcome.

Assume that your goal is, like Phillip's, to be financially independent by a certain age. What are the implications of defining such a goal? For one thing, you have to determine what you mean by being financially independent. Does it mean never having to work again? Does it mean you are your own boss, with a successful business that gives you financial independence? Does it mean winning the lottery?

Once you are clear on what it means to you, define how you intend to achieve the goal. Is it sufficient to plan to work hard? The answer, of course, is both yes and no.

Perhaps you need to re-think the goal so that it gives a clearer sense of where you want to be in five years, and, more importantly, what you believe you can realistically achieve in five years' time. It might be even clearer if you picture in your head a place you want to be: in five years' time I want to be my own boss, with a business that is already in profit and well on the path to becoming self-sustaining. Of course, something is still missing, and that something is simply your vision.

Speak to most successful entrepreneurs and they will endorse the enormous power of goal setting and the value of planning. Some people write their goals down and use the record as a prompt. For others it is sufficient to set the goal and keep it locked inside their brain, never forgotten, always present. Whether on paper or in your head, most people who set themselves targets or goals, like Phillip, consistently achieve them well inside the timeframe they have set themselves.

We could all throw our hands up in the air and claim we don't know how the magic works, but, frankly, that would be rubbish. Of course we know how it works. It works because when we are focused, when we have a clear plan of action, when we have clearly articulated goals with a defined target, when we are driven by an overarching vision of a future place where we want to be, if we have all of that, how can it possibly not work.

# 7

# Visionary leadership

Study after study is devoted to the enduring traits of powerful leadership. Every self-respecting business consultant has a list of leadership attributes on their website. Ideas around leadership are the joy of bloggers.

Thousands of books have been written on the subject, and your bible might be as old as Sun Tzu's *Art of War* or as recent as John Maxwell or Stephen Covey. Each one will find a way to give you the author's special insight into those traits, and when you've put the book down or surfed the net long enough, what you will be left with is a simple truth: every great leader has a clear vision of where their organisation is going.

Now, not everyone defines entrepreneurs as great leaders, but the defining marks of both entrepreneurs and leaders are fundamentally the same.

Great leaders and great entrepreneurs understand that not only must they articulate a clear vision, they must implement it (a vision left hanging without anywhere to go is like Edison inventing the light bulb and then walking away from it before he invents a light fitting and a plug to connect it to).

Phillip Di Bella's mantra is clear:

"Great leaders, and I include people like Branson in that description, have a vision, and the ability to manifest it. And to fulfil the mantle of powerful leadership a vision, and its creator, requires two primary drivers.

The first driver is clarity of purpose. No matter how visionary or how clever the vision is, for it to be a catalyst in effective leadership the vision needs to be sufficiently clear and powerful to arouse someone's interest and engagement.

The second driver is the capacity of the leader to use the vision to instil in everyone involved a level of motivation that is so strong it can empower the organisation to perform at heights never thought possible; a vision so compelling it can focus the energy of people within the organisation to not only believe they can get a result, but that they can achieve outstanding results."

The capacity of an individual to clearly articulate their dream is an amazing gift. The ability to share that dream with others is worth its weight in gold. Too many businesses fail simply because their leader cannot communicate what they want to achieve and how they are going to do it. If they cannot communicate their dream, why should anyone else want to even consider sharing the journey? Part of that ability is in their passion, which Phillip Di Bella shares with so many other successful entrepreneurs. But no amount of empty rhetoric can save a poorly conceived or badly thought through vision.

Depending on how you rate success, Steve Jobs may have already grabbed the honours for a vision that will go down in the annals of history as the most valuable corporate vision ever.

Jobs captured people's imagination when he enthused "There's something going on here ... something that is changing the world, and this is the epicentre." Egotistical, or simply accurate, as Isaacson points out in his biography, Jobs considered Apple his greatest creation, "a place where imagination was nurtured, applied and executed in ways so creative that it became the most valuable company on earth."

Not quite a vision statement, but it starts to set the scene for something most of us would want to be part of.

In essence, Jobs' vision for Apple was focused on the consumer enjoying a completely seamless computing experience. Again, Isaacson sums it up well when he wrote that Jobs wanted "Apple to have end-to-end control of every product that it made. He could not contemplate the idea of Apple software running on another computer, or unapproved apps or content polluting an Apple device".

Integrating hardware and software and content into one unified system enabled Jobs to impose simplicity, which helped him to create enormous customer satisfaction, but that decision also put Jobs firmly on one side of the most fundamental divide in the digital world: open versus closed. Jobs was closed, while Wozniak, in the early days at least, opted for open. In its most simple form the epitome of open was the Apple II, which Wozniak designed with a myriad of slots and ports that people could jack into – heaven for the hobbyist or hacker, but counter to everything Jobs was pushing.

In Jobs' corner sat the Macintosh, designed under strict control from Jobs to ensure it was as closed a system as possible. He fought tooth and nail to keep it that way, reluctantly accepting the barest minimum number of slots while holding out to ensure that the case could only ever be opened by special tools designed by Apple engineers. This vision for seamless end-to-end integration was the catalyst that drove Apple to develop a digital hub strategy to link your desktop computer seamlessly with a range of portable digital devices such as the iPod and iPad. The only catch was that both were part of Apple's closed and tightly integrated system with access only available using Apple's iTunes software and content downloaded from its iTunes Store. He had his customers held hostage, but very few of them complained.

Some commentators argue that Jobs' vision had already been tested and found wanting on the world stage by declaring that the Macintosh operating system would not be available under licence to any other company's hardware. This put him in direct opposition to the Microsoft strategy of allowing anyone prepared to pay the licensing fee to use Windows. The outcome was intriguing. Microsoft became the most dominant player on the world computing stage in operating systems, Apple barely rated. Jobs' vision was never to dominate the world market for operating systems.

When Jobs found himself at odds with the rest of Apple's management, he left. His time at Pixar, and the vision he implemented and the success he achieved as CEO, is another story entirely. But while Jobs was gone, Apple spent a great deal of time in the wilderness. The company struggled to find the single-minded purpose that Jobs was famous for. He may have been contrary, difficult to get on with, but we believe his vision was iron-clad. Apple is where it is today because of Jobs' vision and his obsession with it. He fought for a seamless consumer experience in computing. He won some of the early rounds, but lost some in the middle. When he returned from his time with Pixar, he had more confidence and was a lot smarter. How much smarter? At the time of writing, Apple had become the world's most valuable company. Sales exceeded $100 billion, while the market value had climbed to $337billion, outstripping Microsoft's $202 billion.

There is, however, one leadership trait in which great entrepreneurs can often outshine great leaders, regardless of what title they hold or who they work for. We saw it in Jobs, at Apple. We saw it while Gates was driving Microsoft. We certainly saw it when Henry Ford was implementing his vision.

It's ironic that much of the criticism directed at politicians, particularly the leaders of political parties, is about their failure to establish policies or to articulate a vision that differentiates them from their opponents.

Hawke and Howard have been the only politicians in Australia's recent history who have endured for any significant period, but their ability to differentiate themselves and their parties became blurred as they inevitably moved towards the same goals, driven by the changing demographics within the electorate and their ambition to be re-elected.

Very few of today's politicians seem comfortable with the idea of creating a vision. Even fewer would appear to have the charisma to sell it.

To his supporters, Paul Keating was the last politician to clearly articulate a vision. They point to the Redfern Speech as a clear demonstration of Keating's ability to articulate a vision of what the future could look like, one that could be shared by all Australians.

On the 10th of December 1992, Paul Keating addressed a gathering of largely Indigenous Australians in the Sydney suburb of Redfern. It was a powerful speech and has since earned the accolade as one of the greatest Australian speeches ever. In the view of listeners to ABC Radio National the speech rated as one of the exemplary speeches of all time, alongside Martin Luther King's "I have a dream" speech and Jesus Christ's "Sermon on the Mount".

The occasion was the launch of the 1993 International Year of the World's Indigenous People. On the surface, the speech dealt with the challenges facing Indigenous Australians, and it was the first time an Australian Prime Minister had acknowledged publicly that European settlers were responsible for the difficulties Australian Aboriginal communities continued to face.

Read the entire speech and you will be mesmerised by how clearly Keating was able to articulate his vision for Indigenous Australians. But what astounds most people when they read the transcript of the Redfern Speech is the subtlety used to remind all Australians of the way history has shaped where we stand today, and how history could provide clues on how to realise Keating's vision. This is a short extract, with Keating asking non-Indigenous Australians to consider how they would feel if they were placed in the same position as Indigenous Australians:

... it might help us if we non-Aboriginal Australians imagined ourselves dispossessed of land we have lived on for 50,000 years – and then imagined ourselves told that it had never been ours.

Imagine if ours was the oldest culture in the world and we were told that it was worthless. Imagine if we had resisted this settlement, suffered and died in the defence of our land, and then were told in history books that we had given up without a fight. Imagine if non-Aboriginal Australians had served their country in peace and war and were then ignored in history books. Imagine if our feats on sporting fields had inspired admiration and patriotism and yet did nothing to diminish prejudice. Imagine if our spiritual life was denied and ridiculed.

Imagine if we had suffered the injustice and then were blamed for it. It seems to me that if we can imagine the injustice then we can imagine its opposite. And we can have justice.

Paul Keating was Prime Minister from 1991 to 1996. He was voted out of office, to be replaced by a coalition government lead by John Howard. Since Keating's speech at Redfern, much has changed in the way Indigenous Australians are able to engage in the societal fabric of this country, yet there is still disagreement about government policy and government actions. And the debate is not simply between political factions but within the Indigenous community and the non-Indigenous communities. Was Paul Keating's vision of a future place flawed, or were there other impediments to his ability to see it through?

In *Lazarus Rising*, John Howard's autobiography, published after he left office in 2007, Howard argues that he did not have a new vision for the country. In fact he contends that there is no place for governments to set a vision:

"I had a project for government, but I was not so arrogant as to presume that I should inflict on the Australian people a new vision for the nation. Successive generations had given Australia a good enough vision and a sense of her identity, and I believed in the fundamentals of what I saw around me.

"Good leadership interprets and applies the received values of a nation. In many ways the changes I wished to bring about would more directly echo the instincts of the Australian people, rather than impose on them something new, and about which they would feel uncomfortable."

Who was right? Keating, who outlined a clear vision of what he believed the future of Australia should be like, or John Howard, who rejected as arrogance the right of politicians to set a vision for the country, arguing that he was caretaker, or manager, of the vision set down by previous generations of Australians?

In the context of this book we should applaud Paul Keating for his clarity, his compassion and his eloquence, but did Keating have the capacity to implement a vision that would be decades in the doing?

Consider this, and file it away for future reference. Phillip Di Bella contends that there can only ever be one entrepreneur in an organisation.

"To achieve success a strong leader, perhaps the CEO in a corporation, perhaps the leader of a political party, or the anointed head of a religious body, whoever that leader is, he or she must always be in control of the agenda.

Once they stop being in control, the vision they built their success on must change."

That doesn't mean the company immediately goes into crash mode. Far from it. But the lesson for every entrepreneur is real, and needs to be heeded. A critical part of sharing and driving the vision is the ability of successful entrepreneurs like Phillip Di Bella to create a succession plan for people within the organisation. None of these people can ever replace Phillip in the same way that no one will ever replace Jobs, or Branson. It is not about replacement, but evolution.

While Phillip Di Bella's vision is alive and he is in control, no one can ever take that vision over. The people in the succession plan are part of Phillip's vision, they are the people he trusts to implement the strategies to achieve his vision. In fact Phillip expects each of his directors to define their own vision within his plan, so that they own their part in the journey.

That's how you have to think about vision. It's the end journey; it's the ultimate realisation of your dream. And unlike a goal you won't necessarily know when you've fully achieved it, but that's ok too, because as long as you keep on setting yourself new goals, you will keep on enriching your vision.

# 8

# The power to ignite the globe

If I said to you that the power of your passion could ignite the globe, you would probably scoff or laugh at me. You might even question whether you had passion in you at all; this mystical thing that we are told burns in all of the world's great entrepreneurs; this thing that lights up a person's face when they start talking about their passion. Anyone who ever watched Steve Jobs on stage at an Apple launch will have some sense of the passion that drove the man. Every step was carefully orchestrated, yet Jobs managed to imbue everything he touched with a level of belief that was palpable, and his audience hung on every word.

Richard Branson may not be the same skilled presenter as Jobs was. In fact there are times when Branson appears self-conscious if a microphone is thrust into his hands, yet we defy anyone not to be captivated by the man's self-belief. Try taking the smile off the man's face when he enthuses about every one of his ventures. When he announced his plans to offer space travel to the average millionaire he did so with a look reminiscent of the cat who'd found the spilt cream. It certainly wasn't the look of a smug capitalist who had pulled off another deal, but the look of a man who had poured his life and soul into everything he did.

I've watched Phillip Di Bella speak in public on many occasions. He is one of those fearless public speakers who everyone envies. I once reminded him that there are only two types of public speakers – nervous ones and liars. Phillip laughed.

"When I was nine, my parents celebrated their 25th wedding anniversary. I remember declaring to them at breakfast one morning I was going to make a speech at the party being planned. It never occurred to me to be frightened. I knew what I wanted to say, and the idea of standing up in front of 50 or 60 people wasn't intimidating at all."

Phillip tells the story quietly but with a level of energy that is evident whenever he speaks about things that are important to him. People who were there tell of the confident way he stood in front of the gathering and gave the polished performance of a veteran public speaker, joking and reflecting on his parent's history before congratulating them on their milestone.

Like the late Steve Jobs, Phillip has the ability to share his passion with others. He is a skilled and natural presenter, yet I doubt that he has ever taken lessons in presentation techniques. Likewise, Steve Jobs. Whenever Jobs presented Apple's latest creation at a product launch his performance was peerless because he was articulating on stage the very things he believed in. Not just words written by a gifted speechwriter, but his own words, setting out the absolute purity of everything he had advocated for over four decades. Perhaps the most critical test Tim Cook faced as Steve Jobs' replacement as CEO at Apple was not how he would protect the share price, but whether he could demonstrate to the faithful an ability to match it with Jobs at an Apple product launch. Of course the irony, as we will come to understand through the progress of this book, is that one is an undeniable outcome of the other.

For Phillip Di Bella, his passion is a way of life; it is a natural part of who he is and an essential part of his persona. There is nothing contrived or false about Phillip. You take him as he is, or move on. I've heard people accuse Phillip of getting aggressive, mistaking his passion for something else. Phillip doesn't so much lament these occurrences, but acknowledges how difficult passion is to understand:

"If my voice goes up an octave, someone might point and say, 'Look, Phil's getting aggressive'. But I'm not! Nothing could be further from the truth. A part of being passionate is this bursting, overwhelming feeling that I have to get out."

Phillip points to this as the dichotomy of passion. People can identify passion, or what they perceive as passion, through facial expressions or the gestures of another, but that is a superficial view, some fulfilment of the idea that perception rules the world.

The practised public orator will use their hands to underline the point they are making. They will gesticulate and roam the stage, like the best performers should. But can you discern from their actions their true inner passion?

At best you can say that they present their case with a level of passion, but you will never be able to categorically know whether their performance is a learnt act or a genuine display of their beliefs. Great actors can transport you to a different place, ask you to forget all your beliefs and convince you that black is white, but as soon as you leave the cinema or the theatre, black is black once more.

Passion cannot be contrived. It must be a natural behaviour. But unlike the contrivances of the performer it is not always easy to identify the passion that resides within, or how that passion can transform an idea or turn an opportunity into a multi-million dollar enterprise. Before anyone can employ passion they need to be very clear what it is, how it works and how it transforms. If we can demystify this abstract idea then we can demystify one of the most powerful drivers of successful entrepreneurs the world over.

Ask yourself: what is the essence of this passion?

Or, more to the point, have you ever tried to define passion?

The best sales people in the world will tell you that if you can't define something, you can't sell it. So, if you can't define your own passion, how can you explain what it is to somebody else? More importantly, how can you use that passion to inspire, to create, or as the basis of an idea?

The dictionaries don't help us much. Most define passion as any kind of feeling or emotion, with the rider that it must be an emotion of compelling force. Such a definition starts to get somewhere, but then the dictionaries do what they do best, they confuse the issue by adding choice: Strong amorous feeling of love; passionate sexual love; an instance or experience of it; a person who is the objective of such a feeling; violent action. To add to all this confusion there is also a religious factor aligning passion to beliefs, defining passion as the gospel narrative of the sufferings of Christ or reverence for the Prophet Muhammad.

When a communication audit was carried out at Di Bella Coffee there was a real struggle amongst the staff to articulate the correlation between the core value of passion as a key plank in the company's corporate philosophy and each individual employee's personal perspective on passion. Just as the dictionaries confirm, passion was interpreted by the group in a myriad of ways. To some, passion was a religious word, to others it embodied anger, to others it was at the core of every Mills & Boon romance novel.

Phillip Di Bella adds clarity to the confusion by exploring the different aspects of passion and digging beneath the superficial words and meanings:

"There are two sides to passion – there's the passion that someone perceives, then there's the passion you own – your internal passion. That's where people go wrong – too many people claim they are passionate, but they fail to own it. You have to own passion; you have to know that to you its natural."

The compelling question is, while everyone has a level of passion in them, can you teach someone passion? Most books tell you, quite emphatically, that no, you can't. Phillip Di Bella believes that to even entertain the idea actually dumbs down the premise, just as believing that you can teach entrepreneurship from some kind of prescriptive text book devalues that concept. However, we have come to the conclusion that, like entrepreneurship, you can teach people how to identify their passion.

Implicit in this philosophy is the recognition that how well a person understands their passion effectively determines their capacity to share it. And understanding the power of sharing your passion is fundamental to becoming a great entrepreneur.

# 9

# Never be frightened of passion

The walls of Di Bella Coffee's boardroom are covered with mementos to sporting greats. A huge frame holds a dedication to Muhammad Ali's World Championships. On the coffee table in Phillip's office is a picture book of Ali's exploits. Phillip Di Bella rejects the suggestion that Ali is a hero. To define his admiration for the man he points to Ali's commitment and self-belief. The way Ali confronted and dealt with the very thing that Phillip believes is the Achilles' heel of all potential entrepreneurs: their ability to engage with their passion.

Ali is a living legend. He is recognised and admired by people across the globe, regardless of their religion or their colour. Many of the stories about him have been embellished and retold until they've reached a point where it is difficult to separate the man from the legend.

In his biography *Muhammad Ali – His Life and Times,* Thomas Mauser describes Ali as a superb human being with good qualities, but also with flaws.

> "In his twenties he was arguably the greatest fighter of all time. But more importantly he reflected and shaped the social and political currents of the age in which he reigned. Ali in the 1960s stood for the proposition that principles

mattered, that equality among people was just and proper, and that the war in Vietnam was wrong." [3]

Muhammad Ali's life moved through many phases. Named Cassius Marcellus Clay at birth, he changed his name to Muhammad Ali when he discovered Islam in his twenties. He won the heavyweight boxing title of the world when he was 22. He was sentenced to prison for refusing to be drafted into the army during the Vietnam War because his religious beliefs told him it was wrong to kill others. As a result of his stance, he spent more than three years being denied the right to defend the boxing world championship crown he had deservedly won from Sonny Liston. Surprisingly, respect for him didn't diminish during this time; it grew and grew.

Sitting in Phillip's office, the book of Ali's exploits open in front of us, a picture of Ali facing up to Sonny Liston dominates the page. "The primary suppressor of passion in individuals is fear," Phillip states emphatically. "You see the most passionate people in the world suppressed by fear. You see it on the face of politicians with the polls against them. What makes them turn up to face the media the next day when the public has been clamouring for their removal? They've faced their fear; they've recognised what the worst case scenario is. And the world hasn't ended."

Phillip believes that passionate people are capable of dominating fear, but even the most passionate person will be overcome by fear if they lose their passion or their self-belief and commitment, then they will ultimately lose sight of their outcomes.

Ali, Phillip insists, is the very model of someone passionate about outcomes, someone who has confronted his worst possible scenario and succeeded. But, perhaps, not in the way most people would think.

When Sonny Liston threw in the towel in the seventh round of their title fight, Muhammad Ali danced around the ring, appearing

---

3    *Muhammad Ali His Life and Times*. Thomas Hauser, Open Road Integrated Media, New York.

to levitate, shouting, "I am the greatest! I am the greatest! I'm the greatest! I'm the king of the world! To many people his arrogance jarred, to others he had proven himself a supreme athlete whose confidence was fully justified.

Phillip Di Bella would argue that this is simply fulfilment of Ali's desired outcome:

"The way Ali constructed the outcome he wanted to achieve was deliberate. He may have appeared arrogant enough to claim the outcome before it was fully realised, but his self-belief was paramount. Ali knew what he was doing and what he needed to do. He was careful and deliberate in his tactics."

Ali understood his strengths and weaknesses, inside and outside of the ring. He taunted his opponents before fights by predicting the round when he would knock them out. He had goaded Liston for months, knowing it would make the other boxer angry and want to take the fight up to Ali. He knew he was faster than Liston, that he could tire Liston and turn the fight his way. It was calculated, but it was also predictably strategic. In his dressing room after the fight, Ali understood the need to maintain the momentum of building an impenetrable aura around him. He rounded on the reporters gathered in the room demanding they acknowledge him as the greatest fighter in the world, a fighter who wasn't scared of any opponent on earth. At first they hesitated.

He yelled at them again and again, "Who's the greatest in the world?"

Finally, a number responded. "You are!"

But the man they were calling the greatest in the world, the man who was renowned for being fearless in the lead up to every fight, the so-called Louisiana Lip who taunted his opponents with poems that predicted the end, admitted he was scared of Liston:

"When the referee was giving us instructions, Liston was giving me the stare. And, I won't lie, I was scared. Sonny Liston was one of the greatest fighters of all time. He was one of the most scientific boxers who ever lived. He hit hard, and he was fixing to kill me. It frightened me just knowing how hard he hit."

Fear is a perplexing emotion. Aroused by a perceived threat, fear is a basic survival mechanism that occurs in response to a specific stimulus. When you ask people what it is that sparks their fear of public speaking they will shuffle their feet and stare at the ground. They mumble something about forgetting what it is they are supposed to be saying, that they will lose their place in their notes, or that something will be amiss with their clothing or their hair. When they finally look you in the eye they invariably admit that the perceived threat is what other people will think of their performance, of them.

Public speaking might be a torture for/to some people, a fear worse than death, but it is only one of hundreds of fears that people must identify and confront. Phillip Di Bella defines fear in terms of a person's worst possible scenario because, he argues, that is the most defining moment in their lives.

Let's be clear about what we are getting at here. A few years back, a well-known identity by the name of Bear Grylls hosted a TV program with the title *Worst Case Scenarios*. The program aired on the Discovery Channel, on pay television, and attracted a loyal audience.

Bear Grylls, an American, served in the 21 Regiment Special Air Services (21 SAS) where he learned self-survival skills. The program was based on using those skills to survive man-made disasters and natural cataclysms. The list of episodes read like a person's worse nightmare: escaping from burning cars, being attacked by dogs, a rattlesnake encounter, surviving an earthquake or being trapped in extreme cold, surviving an elevator plunge, an encounter with a tarantula, and, probably the most likely of worst case scenarios Bear Grylls was asked to confront, how to deal with a home break-in.

Each one of the scenarios Grylls was asked to confront occur as part of the business of living and existing. Earthquakes happen, large spiders emerge from under leaves in the garden, the number of lifts that crash from their highest point to the basement can probably be counted on one hand. You either confront those types of worst case scenarios bravely and resourcefully, or they could be the death of you. You react because you have to, regardless of whether you have been fortunate to be taught survival skills or not.

When Phillip Di Bella talks about confronting your worst case scenario, he is defining a moment when the choice is yours, to either confront the situation or not. The outcome then defines, potentially, the turning point in your life. But you have the choice, as Alan Joyce, the CEO of Qantas, confronted when he was faced with a decision to ground an entire airline in order to save it.

For months leading up to October 2011, Alan Joyce had been dealing with ongoing industrial unrest over failed negotiations involving three unions: the Australian Licensed Aircraft Engineers Association (ALAEA), the Australian and International Pilots Association (AIPA) and the Transport Workers Union of Australia (TWU). Commentators and aviation experts were predicting the standoff was cruelling the company's ability to operate profitably.

On the 29th October, Joyce took a decision to ground the entire Qantas domestic and international fleet and took steps to lock out all Qantas union employees. The decision Joyce took had the potential to devastate Qantas, the Qantas share price, the trust of the flying public, even the trust of government. Subsequent reports suggested that the action by Joyce had a daily financial impact of AUD$20 million. Over 68,000 customers were affected across the globe, many were left stranded in airports where they had arrived to catch flights without any inkling of what was about to happen.

In the early hours of 31 October, 2011, Fair Work Australia

ordered that all industrial action taken by Qantas and the involved trade unions be terminated immediately. The order was requested by the federal government amid fears that an extended period of grounding would do significant damage to the national economy, especially the tourism and mining sectors.

It's not really the place of this book to speculate on who won or lost in this confrontation, suffice to say that since that action was taken by Alan Joyce significant changes have occurred within Qantas. No more than 12 months after grounding the entire fleet of planes, Joyce announced a significant code-sharing deal with Emirates, the powerful United Arab Emirates airline. In the process, he confirmed the airline's intention to take a significant change in direction.

The more important question, from our point of view, was whether this was a defining moment in Alan Joyce's career with Qantas? Did his decision confront his worst possible scenario?

Phillip Di Bella believes so.

"You saw fear all over Alan Joyce's face when he called the union's bluff and grounded Qantas. He was facing his worst possible scenario – he'd lose his job, his reputation – he either had the support of the flying public or he was gone. Watch him today – there's no fear on his face. When he fronts media conferences he's relaxed, almost jovial, because he knows he confronted his greatest fear and is now in control."

Phillip contends that failure to confront your greatest fear makes the rest of the exercise pointless, or futile:

"Books like this mean nothing unless you personally are comfortable with your worst possible scenario. No book will create success for you, but there are books that will enable you to identify your worst possible scenario and help you grow from that point."

Phillip is also adamant that when someone confronts their worst possible scenario and becomes comfortable with it, that is the defining moment when a person starts to conjure up their own passion:

> "Identifying your worst possible scenario is critical to unlocking your passion. My first worst case scenario was not getting a job when I left university. When I set up Di Bella Coffee, my worst case scenario was going broke.
>
> Successful entrepreneurs confront their fears constantly, and then deal with them passionately and effectively. When I'm comfortable with my worst possible scenario, like losing my entire despatch team, I'm going to go about fixing it with passion and drive because I'm not fearful of losing them; I have other people who I can put in there.
>
> At the end of the day, the thing that will prevent people who are likely to read this book from realising their potential is fear of the consequences, and their reluctance to confront it."

Late in 2013, Qantas and Joyce were once again in the news.

Joyce had called on the Federal Government to guarantee to stand behind the Qantas debt in a move to contain a potential blow-out in borrowing costs in face of the need to be competitive in a price war instigated by Virgin.

Alan Joyce embarked on a very public campaign to highlight the growing foreign ownership of Virgin, arguing that Qantas was at a significant disadvantage because the Qantas Sale Act, imposed by the commonwealth when it sold Qantas in the 1990s, limited foreign investment in the airline, thereby providing Virgin with greater opportunities to use its off-shore partners to support price-cutting.

In Joyce's own words, "Virgin would be free to continue its anti-competitive strategy aimed at crippling Qantas."[4]

---

4    "Qantas to seek federal aid on debt". *The Australian* Friday, November 29, 2013.

Joyce's demeanour was of a man who had already confronted his worst possible scenario. He had been there before and had, clearly, no fear in going there again.

\*\*\*

When Muhammad Ali admitted to being frightened of the awesome power of Sonny Liston he wasn't only talking about the physical. In regard to the awesome might of Sonny Liston, Ali knew his only course of action was to confront his opponent. "I was there; I didn't have no choice but to go out and fight."

Ali was intuitive enough to understand that fear existed on a number of levels and needed to be confronted in its different guises. He recognised that there was a much more fundamental fear than the power of Liston's punches that could derail his journey.

Months earlier, when asked whether he was worried about fighting Liston, Ali confided:

"Well, I'm like Columbus. I think the world is round, but I'm a little scared because now I'm reaching the point where I'll find out if it's really round and I can sail around it. Or is it flat and will I fall off? I think I can beat him. I think I'm going to do what I say. But I won't know for sure until I get there."

Ali was not just talking about the prospect of being hurt by Liston; he was equating his fear to a much bigger motivation than one fight, or one punch.

Ali's passion evolved from his belief at a very young age that he was destined to do something for his people. At age eight or ten he would leave his home each morning expecting God to issue him with a command, or a direction for him to take. Growing up, he was upset by the number of coloured people who thought it was better to be white, that if they could they would trade their coloured skin for a much lighter shade.

Ali rejected the very basis for racial discrimination, or any notion that blacks were inferior to whites. He became angry when he saw black people allowing themselves to be used by white do-gooders intent on showing some kind of acceptable black version of white. This became his challenge, like Columbus confronting the shape of the earth. Ali was not prepared to accept that black people deserved anything less than to have their equal place in the world, comfortable in the skin God had given them. He was convinced that he could help his people became stronger, but that each step would require another fear to be confronted and dealt with.

The decisions he took were deliberate. Changing his name from Cassius Clay freed him from the identity given to his family by slave masters, but exposed him to the criticism of his own kind, who believed that black should somehow be a coloured version of white, and while taking the name Muhammad Ali committed him to his beliefs, in the eyes of the American public it also put him at risk of being vilified as an outspoken crusader for a minority religion. With each decision, Ali was confronting another worst possible scenario because of his passionate belief that black Americans deserved better than they got. When he evoked his religious beliefs to refuse to be drafted into the army, what was the worst thing that could happen to him? Would the authorities send him to jail? Would he lose the right to defend his world championship? More importantly, did that matter?

So, from a young age Ali was already fighting a much more important fight than any he had in the ring, and it is a credit to him that many believe only Martin Luther King had more influence over changes to racial discrimination than he did.

Phillip Di Bella is quick to point out that most of us will never have to confront a worst case scenario of the scale that could change a nation. Most of us deal with fears at a much less confronting level. However, he is also adamant that the lesson is universal and the outcome is predictable when people allow fear to suppress their passion:

"I see it when people come in to be interviewed for a job. One person I knew had applied for a position with Di Bella Coffee. He's normally jovial and excited. He came in very subdued, unlike his usual self. So I asked, 'What is the worst possible thing that could happen to you?' He replied, 'That you don't like me and get rid of me in six months.' I asked him if he really believed that it was me who controlled that, or him. When he realised that the security of his job was in his control, that it was up to him to perform, the energy was back and the fear was gone."

Although going broke may have been the worst possible scenario Phillip confronted when he started up Di Bella Coffee, he is not frightened of going broke.

"I don't make decisions to go broke, but if everyone stopped drinking coffee tomorrow I'd get a well-paid job using my skills. Maybe I could sit on boards. There are endless opportunities. If that's my worst case scenario, then I've already confronted it and I'm energised by it."

Think back to the last time you were forced to confront a fear or deal with something that had been worrying you. When you dealt with it, how did you feel? Energised or disappointed. Uplifted or depressed. Phillip Di Bella's point is very clear: identifying your worst case scenario is the start to unlocking your passion, and to unlocking your true potential. What is it that you are most fearful about? What is your worst case scenario? What's holding you back from unlocking your passion?

# 10

## Unlocking your passion

Passion is one of the most infectious things on this planet because while passion may belong to an individual its benefit can spread to an entire organisation. The power of an individual's passion may start by only spreading to a few, but, carefully nurtured, it can spread much wider. It could be argued that this is intuitive, that we all understand this, but I'm not so sure. Essentially, how we capitalise on the infectiousness of individual passion effectively separates the great entrepreneurs from the rest.

The passion of successful entrepreneurs drives them to achieve. Yet their passion may not be what you think it is.

You see passion in the eyes of successful sportsmen and women driven to achieve, not because of the money but because they want to climb their particular Everest. Whenever Greg Norman teed up on the golf course there was a glint in his eye that had nothing to do with the lure of gold if he won. From his first days as a young professional, Norman was passionate about succeeding: "I always wanted to be the best I could be at whatever I did. I didn't want to be the number one golfer in the world. I just wanted to be as good as I could be."

Whether he wanted to be or not, Norman was number one golfer in the world for a staggering 331 weeks. Except for Tiger Woods, no other golfer has ever achieved such an outstanding record. Norman, like Woods, was not just determined to be the best – he was passionate about being the best.

Great entrepreneurs know that sharing their passion will engage others. Jobs understood it, which is why he poured his heart and soul into every Apple presentation; Branson shares his passion of 'doing' with everyone who works with him, to ensure the success of Virgin. A select number of politicians have been able to share their passion in a way that could inspire nations. John F Kennedy did it; Mao Zedong unified the Chinese; even those who have not realised all they have promised, such as Barack Obama and Gough Whitlam, have still captured the essence of their passion and shared it with millions of people.

Passion belongs to the individual, but the power of passion is that it is so infectious that it can ignite a globe. Yet many people doubt they have the necessary passion to do things. Phillip Di Bella's response to that uncertainty is unequivocal.

"How do you know? How can you know you don't have something if you can't describe it? If you can't immediately write down what passion means to you, if you don't know what it means to you, how can you say you don't have passion?"

This is the crunch question. So, what is your passion, and how do you identify it? And the answer, when you find it, may surprise you.

The title of Richard Branson's book *Screw it, Let's do* it captures the essence of the man's passion, and it is hard to ignore it when it oozes out of his pores every time he discusses one of his ventures or deeds.

"I have always lived my life by thriving on chances and adventure. The motive that drives me has always been to set myself challenges and try to achieve them."

But how do you define *your* passion?

Phillip Di Bella believes that too many people spend a lifetime trying to articulate their own passion by looking in the wrong places.

"Men and women who spend decades in a profession wrongly believe their passion is their profession – law, medicine – or their industry – tourism, advertising." (He adds the last comment with a wink in my direction.)

"Think in these terms and you are defining your own passion in a way that will never allow you to unlock the real passion within."

Phillip's observation is insightful. I spent nearly three decades in the advertising business. I wasn't passionate about the advertising game. What became clear to me was that I was passionate about helping people find clarity. I spent years writing advertising briefs on behalf of clients who didn't know how, or who failed to apply a single-minded ruthlessness to what was required. Discovering my passion was like a dam bursting. People had often turned to me to help them discover their own clarity, their own level of objectivity and single-mindedness. I had a gift that others lacked. Yet I had undervalued it, treated it as simply another asset, like intelligence. When I finally opened my eyes and realised what my passion was, it ignited my globe and opened up opportunities that I never realised existed.

Steve Jobs did not start Apple with Steve Wozniak because he was passionate about technology or, for that matter, computers. Read Isaacson's biography on Jobs and you will soon discover a man who was passionate about what he did, but passionate about 'what' is a much harder question for Isaacson to answer.

Jobs was a complex, but brilliant, man. His mother taught him to read before starting school. He was intellectually special and associated with the other smart kids. He quickly became bored at school and was often in strife. He was suspended and threatened with expulsion for his love of practical jokes.

He was fascinated by maths, science and electronics, indulging his interests by building electronic gadgets and hanging out with engineers. He started smoking marijuana at the age of 15 and is reported to have been experimenting with LSD in his senior year at high school. In his spare time he liked to work, but could not be pinned down. As a kid he'd worked a paper round, as a teenager he installed nuts and bolts on frequency counters at Hewlett-Packard, and worked behind the counter of an electronics parts business.

No one would ever call Jobs an academic; he disliked the tedium of university and dropped out during his first year. Interestingly, instead of fleeing the campus, he stayed on, grew his hair long, exchanged his shoes for sandals and continued to attend class as an unaccredited student. Surprisingly, the college faculty indulged him. He also displayed a fascination with the East and the mystics, eating his meals where he could get hand-outs, including the local Hare Krishna temple. He also spent a great deal of his time at a commune just north of San Francisco exploring his spiritual self.

Wozniak and Jobs became friends around the time when Jobs took his part-time job at Hewlett-Packard. Wozniak, five years older than Jobs, was working on the development of a mainframe computer. The pair shared an almost obsessive love of pranks and music. Wozniak was in seventh heaven. Here was a self-confessed computer geek, a computer and electronics whiz, doing what he was passionate about: developing computer hardware and having the time of his life playing electronic practical jokes on his friends.

The pair hung out in their spare time, scheming and inventing. They developed a gadget they called the Blue Box, which gave them access to free long distance phone calls by replicating the tones that routed signals on the American telecom network AT&T. Like much of what they contrived together, it was used for fun and to play pranks. Once they attempted to pose as Henry Kissinger, long time US Secretary of State, in a phone call to the Pope. Astutely, the bishop at the Vatican who took the call determined that the person on the other end of the phone was a woeful impersonator of the real man and refused to connect them to His Holiness.

111

Undaunted by their unimpressive acting ability, Jobs was still scheming, this time how to turn their Blue Box into more than a hobby. Jobs priced each component in the gadget and came up with a figure of $40. He persuaded Wozniak that they could sell the unit for $150, a smart profit to say the least. Wozniak had an almost pathological dislike of all things business and was perfectly happy leaving the entrepreneurial thinking to Jobs.

Together, they did the rounds of various college dorms and sold more than 100 of the units to college kids who saw the opportunity to ring mum and dad for free as manna from heaven, freeing up untold wealth for more important purchases.

It became clear to those around them that while Wozniak was the computer wizard, Jobs was the one who would figure out how to make the idea user friendly, put it together in a package, market it and make a profit.

Both respected the other. Steve Wozniak summed up their partnership: "Every time I'd design something great, Steve (Jobs) would find a way to make money for us."

Jobs was more forthright, displaying his ability to be almost cruel in his observations of others: "Woz is very bright in some areas, but he's almost like a savant, since he was so stunted when it came to dealing with people he didn't know. We were a good pair."

Although in awe of Wozniak's engineering wizardry, it never prevented Jobs from challenging almost everything that Wozniak designed. They fought over the number of ports the early Apple computers should feature. Wozniak fought for an open system, Jobs wanted it closed.

On and on the debate would rage. In the end it became clear that you could sum up Steve Wozniak's passion with the words 'engineering wizardry'. For Steve Jobs the summation would be something completely different.

As the Apple story unfolded, and Jobs left and then came back, it became clear that what Steve Jobs was passionate about was a seamless customer experience with each and every Apple product. His level of commitment to achieving his vision bordered on the obsessive. He was renowned for needing to control almost every detail to ensure that consumers enjoyed an Apple product experience. Pick up an iPad or an iPhone, touch an iMac, and the experience is almost surreal. That it is different is because of Jobs' passion to be different and to produce truly great, inspiring products.

In the last chapter of Walter Isaacson's biography he quotes Jobs' own definition of his passion:

"My passion has been to build an enduring company where people were motivated to make great products. Everything else was secondary. Sure it was great to make a profit, because that was what allowed you to make great products. But the products, not the profits, were the motivation."

Phillip Di Bella is one of the most knowledgeable, if not the most knowledgeable, person on coffee in this country. For nine years he worked at his father-in-law's café, the Cosmopolitan, in Brisbane's Fortitude Valley. Cosmo was one of the few places in town with a reputation for good coffee amongst the locals. Phillip applied himself to everything that went on about coffee. He learned where to get beans, how to buy them and how to roast them. At the same time, he developed first-class people skills. He insisted that the customer should always come first, and made sure that everyone knew it. Phillip became an expert on the business of coffee and earned a reputation with customers as a craftsman. Along the way, he made tens of thousands of espressos.

But coffee is not Phillip Di Bella's driving passion. When Phillip spoke at his parent's 25th wedding anniversary, he delivered a speech that was well-structured, well-crafted and very passionate. At the very heart of that speech was his passion, and his passion as a nine-year-old was his love for his parents.

Today, his love for his parents is undiminished, while the passion of Phillip Di Bella the entrepreneur exists on an entirely different plane. "My driving passion was never coffee. Sure, coffee is a part of it, but my real passion is opportunity. When I worked at my father-in-law's café, I became passionate about the opportunities I could see around me, which he wouldn't take up. I also became passionate about the level of waste, and I became passionate about the way people were treated."

Phillip's insight into his own passions provides the most important clue yet about passion. To Phillip Di Bella, passion is a behavioural trait where someone feels energised towards an outcome. He argues that coffee is not an outcome; coffee is a part of his journey, but it is not the journey.

So let's consider each in turn.

Firstly, Phillip is passionate about people missing an opportunity, like the opportunities that he believed his father in-law missed out on at the Cosmopolitan. Phillip refuses to waste an opportunity until he has explored every part of it to see whether he can make it work. He shares this side of his passion with everyone he meets by urging them to push to the very limit of their capacity, to explore their own opportunities.

Secondly, Phillip is passionate about the way people are treated, or mistreated, as the case may be. I've never heard him knowingly denigrate or speak ill of anyone. He openly trusts others, unless they damage that trust, yet he will unflinchingly expose vanity, selfishness or narcissistic behaviour if it has the potential to damage the people he cares about or the projects he is committed to. His desire to create the best possible customer experience at Di Bella Coffee is a key part of the demonstrable way he delivers on his passion for how people are treated. Don't ever believe the theory that customers are always right. They're not! But they deserve to be accorded the respect as if they are.

Ensuring that the customer experience is faultless is a key plank in Phillip's brand strategy. But it is not a contrived part of the strategy; something that is such an integral part of your passion cannot be contrived, and it is this which makes it so powerful. To be 'an employer of choice' is one of the five platforms of the company's strategic plan. Phillip and his executive team work hard at ensuring people *want* to work at Di Bella Coffee, and the company implements well-considered workforce development programs to provide all employees with incentives and career paths to encourage them to grow with the company. This is not simply lip-service to a taught ethos but is an integral part of Phillip's makeup, and, as a result, he and the company are rewarded with people's loyalty.

The third part of Phillip's passion is about learning and evolution. Not just a one dimensional passion to satisfy his own hunger for knowledge but a multi-faceted commitment to the belief that continuous learning is an essential part of everyone's development. Phillip openly encourages mentoring. His succession plan for Di Bella Coffee identifies gaps in the knowledge and experience of each executive, and calls for a strategy of mentoring or training to plug the gap. His appointment to the position of Adjunct Professor in Entrepreneurship at Griffith University comes as no surprise to anyone who understands his passion for learning.

As part of his journey he had to become passionate about business, and passionate about coffee, but his measure, the three things that Phillip ties everything back to, is chiselled in bedrock: opportunity, people and learning.

What are you passionate about? Could you sit down with a pen and a piece of paper and identify your passion? Or do you think you would need help?

Every time Phillip and I sat down to discuss this book the conversation would invariably focus on the need for this to be a practical learning opportunity. There is no such thing as an easy solution. Phillip has lost count of the number of people who come up to him at a conference and want to shake his hand. He watches his audience carefully, taking particular note of those who are truly engaged, and those who use the time to send text messages. It amuses him because many of the texters, who paid scant attention during his presentation, will come up and shake his hand, perhaps in the expectation that some of his success might rub off.

You can't buy Richard Branson's passion, or Steve Jobs'. You can't own someone else's passion; you have to discover your own. You can share someone's passion, but it must first and foremost be your passion. What successful entrepreneurs can do, Phillip Di Bella believes, is inspire passion:

> "When I get up to speak at a function I want to inspire someone to do something different. I want to give them the authority to feel amazing about something. Passion is what makes us feel amazing about something."

Phillip is emphatic when he differentiates between passion and inspiration. Passion is within you. Someone speaking passionately doesn't transfer their passion to you but, rather, inspires you to unlock your own passion:

> "People have to open their own passion cabinet. Only the individual can unlock their passion. Great leaders may inspire them to do so, but they can't do it for them."

When you get to the very heart, this is the truth of it, and it comes in two parts. The first part is that you have to be the one who unlocks your passion. No one else can do it for you. Great leaders can inspire you to look for the key, but they can't physically turn it in the lock.

The second part is that you have to believe there is something to unlock. We reject the notion that some people don't have passion in them. The blockage is not the lack of passion, the blockage is more likely the lack of confidence most people have in believing.

In some ways it is very difficult to get the flow of these concepts into the right order. Does self-belief come before you can identify your passion? Does passion help you build your self-belief? The answer, of course, is yes! This is truly a case of the chicken and the egg.

Passion is within you. Your passions may change and evolve, but only you can identify your passion, and only you can use your passion to engage others. Of course the question that won't go away until we have a satisfactory answer is: how do you identify your own passion?

For some, it is as simple as acknowledging a skill you are good at. Sportsmen regularly turn a part-time pastime into a professional passion. Analysing their decision a little further brings you to the question of whether their passion is self-motivated. Do they turn professional because they are encouraged to, because they want to, or a combination of both? Greg Norman started out in golf when he was already well into his teens. As soon as he began playing, he realised where his passion was and how he could realise it. Tiger Woods is reported to have first picked up a golf club when he was three years old. Did he realise at that age what he would become passionate about or did he follow the guidance of his father who has been credited with much of Tiger's early commitment?

If you were asked to define the passion that drove Albert Einstein, or Lee Iacocca, the legendary President of the Chrysler Motor Corporation, or Rupert Murdoch, Chairman of News Corporation, what would your reply be?

If you guessed that Einstein's passion was focused on discovery, you are very close. He once said: "I have no special talents. I am only passionately curious."

Lee Iacocca wasn't quite as creative but, nevertheless, was very pointed when he said, "I loved cars. I couldn't wait to get to work in the morning."

No surprises with Rupert Murdoch, although his response may not sound so unequivocal: "Communicating news and ideas, I guess ... is my passion."

The penultimate word on this surely belongs to Roman

Abramovich, who, after making his billions as part of the Russian oligarchy, moved to live in London. Long before becoming the owner of the Chelsea Football Club in the English Premier League, he is reputed to have said: "I love this game. I love this sport. I love this league. Why don't I get my own team?"

What are you passionate about?

Ask yourself, do you carry a torch for an inequity in the world – perhaps a social injustice or a political irregularity that has sparked your ire, or your intrigue? Do you have a particular skill that eclipses every other interest, or one that you constantly turn to for enjoyment? A hobby can be the source of a passion so powerful it demands more and more of your time, and gets it. What do you do then? Turn away from it, as if a hobby could be no more than a passing fad, or no more deserving of your attention than a weekend guilt trip? Think about what energises you – all of us turn to the things we love doing first. Instead of being another source of guilt, embrace it, understand it. Think about how you can turn it into a business opportunity.

Perhaps your passion hasn't yet emerged, or, like my own experience, you are still struggling to define exactly what it is. Don't despair just yet. Take heart from what Phillip Di Bella argued earlier in this chapter, that passion is within all of us – it might change and evolve but the key to unlocking your passion is to be able to define exactly what it is.

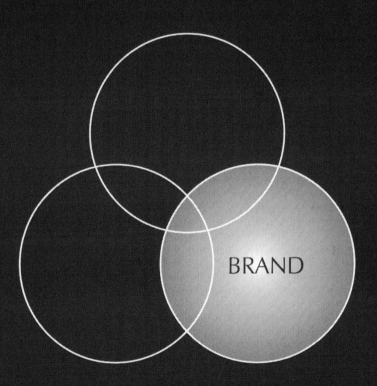

# 11

# Without a customer

In the first two parts of the formula for Entrepreneurial Intelligence we focused on the 'what' and the 'why'. The clarity and power of a vision is essential to establish a direction – the what, that future place we need to be able to see. Passion provides the drive and energy to engage with a purpose, and the capacity to sustain a level of commitment to that purpose to the very end. Yet, as important and powerful as they both are, neither part can provide us with the 'how', which is why we must move on to the third part of the formula.

Without the 'how' the formula can't exist; without the 'how' the formula is like the elements in the petri dish – nothing happens until you add all the critical parts. But, when you do – bang! The reaction occurs, the fizzing starts, the catalyst is there to unlock the opportunity and consume all the doubters.

The 'how' defines a process, or a structure, to implement the necessary strategies that will get you to where you need to be.

The 'how' provides a framework that won't falter under the intensity of your commitment.

The 'how' provides the necessary platform to connect with the market or customer need. And the most powerful way to connect with the customer need is by applying the same strategies that drive every successful brand.

One of the most insightful business commentators of the past century has been Peter Drucker. He is regarded as one of the leading thinkers and writers to ever put pen to paper about management theory and practices.

Drucker died in 2005, leaving a legacy for managers and business owners that may never be equalled. He predicted many of the major developments in business in the second half of the 20th century, including privatisation and decentralisation; he foresaw the rise of Japan as an economic world power; he foretold the emergence of the information society; and he wrote constantly about the power of marketing.

One of Drucker's most memorable quotes occurred when he admonished corporate leaders with the observation that "without a customer, you don't have a business". He constantly expanded and fine-tuned this thought into a customer and market-focused philosophy that had at its core the idea that the only "valid definition of business purpose is to create a customer".

Regardless of the type of business you consider setting up, there is not one single exception to this rule. Want to set up a charity? – you need customers; a business in one of the service sectors? – you need customers. Setting up an online retail operation, a wholesale operation, or even if you want to start growing hydroponic tomatoes – you need customers.

And what are customers if not the very essence of marketing?

Pick up most books on the subject of marketing and you will find a quote from Drucker. Commentators, authors, in fact any student of marketing recognises the value of the practical approach Drucker applied. "Without a customer you don't have a business" is so transparently obvious that you wonder why it isn't emblazoned across every marketing executive's forehead to enshrine the importance of their roles. Drucker, simply, got it, and when he argued that the aim of marketing is to know and understand the customer so well that the product or service sells itself, he was stating the obvious, that, essentially, the business of marketing is the business of building brands. At the heart of that definition is the understanding that marketing is about fulfilling human needs, and that brands have assumed the most powerful place in resolving those needs.

The business of fulfilling human needs is a complex notion that has made many of the same publishers we referred to earlier wealthy by filling book after book with different theories. Perhaps the most famous is Maslow's *Hierarchy of Needs,* which sought to explain the levels of motivation that determine why different people place different emphasis on different needs. Maslow argued that human needs are arranged in a hierarchy from the most pressing to the least pressing.

Different people have different needs, but all people, Maslow argued, try to satisfy the most pressing needs first, and then move up the layers of the hierarchy as each need is resolved. At their most basic, Maslow identified physiological needs, such as hunger and thirst. They are followed by safety, then social needs, esteem and, finally, at the very top of the hierarchy, self-actualisation.

Cavemen satisfied their physiological needs by hunting animals for food and camping by rivers for water. These were commodities at their most basic. Of course, as soon as the food is packaged and sitting on the supermarket shelf, or water from a fancy spring in France is put in labelled bottles, they cease being commodities and become brands. They might still be used to fulfil a person's basic physiological needs, but it is more likely that they are purchased when someone is looking to fulfil their need for recognition or status. In other words, the brand of fancy French water has moved up three rungs on Maslow's hierarchy of needs.

Which brings me full circle to: without a customer … or, more to the point, without a loyal customer … you don't have a business.

Phillip Di Bella contends that understanding what makes customers loyal to your brand is critical to the principles of entrepreneurial intelligence.

"One of the most important lessons anyone can learn is that once you have a customer you need to hold onto them. You don't want to be constantly investing hard-earned funds in winning, and then losing, customers only to have to move on to winning a completely new group."

And the only way to stop customers shopping around is to focus on two core principles: having a better understanding than your competitors about what your customer's need, and developing and implementing strategies that make sure you continually deliver on that need so that they remain loyal. And that leaves us inescapably in the domain of **Brand**.

\*\*\*

Customer loyalty is a complex notion. In your business you might not call them customers; they could be buyers, shoppers or clients. Whatever way you describe them, one thing is crystal clear, your customers, clients, shoppers or buyers will demonstrate potentially different levels of loyalty to your product or service than they might to another product category. The reasons and circumstances will vary.

Loyalty faces a much greater challenge, for example, the more removed you are from your customers. Or you may be involved in a product category that is more price sensitive than others. It is not uncommon for customers of certain products to switch between different brands almost entirely on price. You see them in the supermarkets: shoppers who have already identified three or four brands as able to satisfy their need. Their final decision will be to choose the brand that is on special.

Nor is this type of buying behaviour just restricted to the supermarket. Older buyers may be prepared to consider three or four different brands of clothing. Each of the brands on their list is acceptable in terms of looks, durability, comfort and so forth, so the ultimate decision is which garment has the more attractive price tag.

Another group of customers may be satisfied with your brand and will buy because there is no real motivation to buy a competitor's product. They are not overtly brand loyal; they simply lack the motivation to go elsewhere. They are neither satisfied, nor dissatisfied. They are also expensive to recruit because they require a deal of effort to locate them, and, once located, they will require some incentive to change – an incentive that will cost YOU money. There are different variations on this theme but the heavy cost to convert them is universally the same.

So, from the perspective of entrepreneurial intelligence, how can you improve the odds?

Assuming that nobody disputes Peter Drucker's maxim that without a customer, you don't have a business, how do you build loyalty so that those customers come back again and again and again? We believe the answer is through such a powerful emotional connection with your brand that your customers will never contemplate being disloyal and breaking that connection, in fact they will feel guilty about doing so.

Before you start thinking this is straightforward or easy, ask one of your customers to pin down the exact reason why they purchase, why they remain loyal, and they will struggle to do so. They might suggest that their loyalty is the result of a long association, but longevity on its own doesn't satisfactorily resolve the issue of loyalty. Price has already been rejected as sufficiently strong an incentive, and, anyway, price is not an emotional connection.

Every branded product or service has a long list of pragmatic, functional benefits. It might be something to do with strength or colour, perhaps a list of ingredients that are essential to the makeup of all products in the category. In understanding your customer's need you will already have identified these key factors. At one point in time, Volvo differentiated its cars from every other manufacturer on the benefit of safety. Today, safety is a prerequisite feature or attribute of every motor car, a fact that has forced Volvo to look elsewhere for the emotional linchpin it must find in its branding.

Look in your wardrobe, look around your home, consider the shoes on your feet, the computer on your desk. Consider the iPhone or iPad you use each day – or maybe your loyalty is to another type of tablet or smart phone. Ask yourself why you chose the brand you are using. The answer, if you are honest with yourself, will go some way to identifying the emotional connection you have with that particular brand; some of the way, mind you, not necessarily the whole way.

This is the emotional power of a brand at both its most exciting and it's most irrational. The people with this level of loyalty are the customers every organisation aims to lock away forever; these are the committed customers who wear their pride in the brand as a badge.

There have been some high profile examples of demonstrable pride that may surprise you. In the days when cigarette smoking was socially acceptable, smokers went so far as to display their brand as an expression, or extension, of their own personality. Cigarette packets were left on display on a desk, or a coffee table, or proffered around for the very important reason of establishing the smoker's bona fides. Marlboro smokers responded to the appeal and power of the Marlboro Man advertising campaign, which kept the intended macho image alive for more than four decades. Peter Stuyvesant was the only cigarette to smoke if you were a sophisticated, worldly traveller (or wannabe), and Winfield reminded every Australian that it was ok to be Australian.

Motor cars are high on the list of products that act as a badge of identity, particularly for men, although product diversification has seen the number of female branded vehicles increase exponentially over recent years, with a corresponding rise in the brand loyalty women display toward their car. Bottled beer is another badge male's wear, and is a key part of the strategy that has resulted in imported beer labels taking an increasing share of the market.

Gucci handbags are in the same territory for women, alongside a host of long-standing fashion labels such as David Lawrence and emerging labels like Stella McCartney and Kardashian.

Regardless of the product category, these customers are the most powerful "brand ambassadors" a company can have. Their loyalty guarantees repeat purchase, and their emotional engagement with the brand means they are the most likely to recommend their brand to friends and colleagues.

Phillip Di Bella has an intuitive recognition and understanding of the power of customer loyalty to his brand. "Every morning I went to the Farmers' Markets in New Farm I made sure I had plenty of coffee. But I wasn't going there to sell coffee; I was going there to understand the kind of customer experience I needed to build brand loyalty. When customers started asking me if I would be there next time, I knew my strategy was on track."

In simple business terms, brand loyalty reduces Phillip Di Bella's costs, including his marketing costs.

"The old saying is true – it is cheaper to retain existing customers than it is to get new ones. When I knock on the door of any one of my wholesale customers, the owners of the cafes and restaurants, I have a pretty clear picture in my head of their level of loyalty to Di Bella Coffee. I also know they will require a substantial reason to switch brands. That doesn't make me cocky or over confident, but there is always an inherent risk in anyone changing their brand. Smart operators understand the impact it could have on their customers, so the motivation to switch has to be powerful.

"I am passionate about building relationships so that my customers have little reason to be dissatisfied. I want them to be comfortable with that relationship. It may sound patronising, but it is cheaper to keep a customer happy than it is to try to acquire new ones."

Phillip also knows that it is harder for his competitors to entice his customers to change if they are brand loyal.

> "I work hard on the loyalty of my customers because it then becomes a substantial barrier to entry for my competitors. If a customer is loyal to one brand, you have to throw a lot of money and resources at trying to get them to change."

The logic of what Phillip says is indisputable. It takes a lot of effort to change brands. When people are loyal to a brand, they are buying largely with their heart. They have put a lot of themselves into the decision to choose your brand. They may have been persuaded by friends initially, but after a while the decision becomes theirs alone. The more they use your product, the more they develop positive attitudes towards your product, such that it becomes harder and harder for them to change brands, particularly if they have recommended your brand to some of their friends.

Phillip is also pragmatic about the strength of people's loyalty:

> "They will forgive you one mistake - they may even forgive you a second, but don't push for a third. As much as their ego and their pride may be locked up in this intangible called brand loyalty, most people will only tolerate your ineptitude so far, and then they vote with their feet."

There is an added complication in the way in which Di Bella Coffee needs to define and view its customers. Di Bella Coffee is a manufacturer, a wholesaler and a retailer. That means Di Bella Coffee has to satisfy, and keep satisfied, a number of different motivations and needs, from a range of different customers. There's the café owner who Di Bella Coffee supply with roasted coffee beans; there's the customer sitting at home who can order a kilo of coffee online for personal use; there's the customer who turns up to Di Bella Coffee's drive-thru, or visits one of Di Bella

Coffee's roasting warehouses for a regular morning caffeine fix; and there's the consumer sitting in a café or restaurant somewhere drinking Di Bella coffee. What is common to all of them is that by focusing on the customer experience the brand has the capacity to drive improved business performance. For Phillip, this was where his intuitive understanding of the power of brands merged with his business acumen and the dogmas of accounting and human resources.

The diversity of Phillip's customer base adds another dimension to the question of brand loyalty. In marketing terms, there is a definable distinction between customers and consumers, which can be dealt with very easily. A customer is the person who buys the product; a consumer is the person who consumes, or uses, it. The distinction is clear: mum buys the baked beans for her discerning young son. Her young son, Johnny, nominates the baked beans he prefers on the recommendation of his equally discerning, seven-year-old friend, Simon. Or, if the truth be told, both these discerning young boys have been influenced by the ads they've seen for a particular baked bean on television. Of course, mum may be both the customer and the consumer if she joins Johnny in a breakfast of baked beans on toast.

The list of products impacted in this way covers a wide spectrum of categories. Breakfast cereals are a classic case in point, particularly products that have a high sugar content. The purchase dynamic is complex because, while the child wants to influence the purchase mum makes, mum may not be inclined to purchase the child's preferred choice. Mum will naturally be keen to purchase a product that has nutritional value, but this may not be compatible with the child's choice of a high sugar content cereal. Equally, her initial rejection of the same product may be softened by the knowledge that the child will be more amenable to consuming the product, even though it has less nutritional value.

This is the conundrum faced by every intelligent entrepreneur, not just manufacturers of cereal products. In the case of the cereal manufacturer their decision must weigh up the different customer (or consumer) needs. On the one hand, they know that mum will make the ultimate decision, and, as long as their strategy is not reliant on pester power, they understand that the child will be an influencer on mum's decision. So, do they produce a high sugar content cereal to appease the child or reduce the amount of sugar and please mum? As we said – complex!

Brand loyalty is not one-dimensional. A similar dynamic confronting the cereal manufacturer occurs across the different customer sectors engaged by Di Bella Coffee. Customers loyal to a particular café may have made that choice based on the availability of Di Bella Coffee. Others may do so because the location is convenient, or because the food is always fresh. Only one thing is guaranteed: loyal, satisfied customers will spread the word. They talk to their work colleagues, the friends joining them for a quick lunch break, the visitors from interstate. If their referral is based on the great coffee the café serves, then the value of the Di Bella Coffee brand goes up a notch in what is generally referred to as brand equity.

You will see and hear the term 'brand equity' in a number of different guises. At its very heart, brand equity is the term used to describe the value of a brand. But what does that mean? Essentially, you brand a product or service so that you can charge more than the generic product, which presumes that the brand has more value, but why?

Brand equity is also used to define the value of the brand to a company as an asset, or one of the factors that can be used to evaluate the true worth of a company on the market.

To our way of thinking, the idea of brand loyalty and the term brand equity are indistinguishable, almost interchangeable. The experts may not agree with us, but the best demonstration of a customer's value to a brand is surely in the number of repeat purchases that customer makes, or how many friends they persuade to buy the brand. Whether they pay more for a brand is a demonstration of the perceived extra value the brand represents to the customer. Whether they pay more a second time is a demonstration of the ability of the brand to deliver on the promise implicit in that extra value. Loyalty, therefore, delivers a complete outcome.

In the first chapter, we described how the English adman Stephen King distinguished a product from a brand:

> "A product is something that is made in a factory; a brand is something that is bought by a customer. A product can be copied by a competitor; a brand is unique. A product can be quickly outdated; a successful brand is timeless."

So, what is this concept called 'brand' and how can *you* create the kind of emotional connection great brands achieve? Or, to ask the question a different way, how can your brand contribute to your success in applying entrepreneurial intelligence?

# 12

## This thing called brand equity

Defining brand is not an easy task, building an emotional connection with your customers through your brand is an even more complex web to weave. All of the so-called brand experts have a slightly different take on it, even though they all finish up in much the same place as Stephen King. Unfortunately, that doesn't mean that the definition is simple or, as so many people seem to think, that the sum total of a brand is a name or a logo, or perhaps a combination of the two things. That's why I get enormous satisfaction watching people's faces at the exact point in time when they grasp the full potential power of a brand – that wonderful aha moment when the fog lifts and there's a new convert.

Phillip Di Bella's appreciation of the power of brands to build customer loyalty shows the intuitive understanding intelligent entrepreneurs have about the power of brands. And this is not simply an intangible notion. Phillip understands that his brand is one of the most valuable assets he owns, an asset that is right there on his balance sheet. More and more big business operators and investors are switching on to the growing evidence that a brand can be a company's most valuable asset. Phillip points to those accounting firms who have complex formulas to assess the intangible wealth that brand equity adds to the market value of a company, all because of the loyalty of customers.

Brand Equity, or the idea of a brand as an intangible asset for a company, is not a new idea, but the capacity and wherewithal to calculate such an intangible is.

The first widely reported case of brand equity being used as an asset occurred in 1988 when Phillip Morris purchased Kraft for six times what that company was worth on paper. The sceptics and non-believers thought the management and board of Phillip Morris were completely mad. In fact, far from being mad, they were trailblazers; the management and the board understood perfectly the future returns the Kraft brand would deliver on their investment.

This concept and the understanding of the brand concept have been evolving for centuries. The decision by Phillip Morris was a major milestone in that evolution, forcing accountants the world over to re-think the way they calculated intangible assets. Today, the brand value or brand equity of the top global brands is openly reported by two companies, Interbrand and Millward Brown, who annually publish independent Top 100 Brand lists.

The three top brands in Interbrand's 2013 Top 100 Global Brands report are listed as Apple, Google and Coca Cola. Their combined brand value is shown as a mind boggling US$270 billion. This amount is nothing to do with the tangible assets of each company, which, in Di Bella Coffee, include the exclusive roasting equipment in each of the company's roasting warehouses, the stock on hand and the containers of coffee already on the ocean. Tangible assets also include real estate and the merchandising equipment Di Bella Coffee provides to café and restaurant owners.

These are all assets that can be valued and reported against, whereas intangible assets are more complex. Most people understand the concept of 'goodwill', shown as an intangible asset in the balance sheet only able to be realised when the business is sold. Goodwill is usually shown by a figure representing the original cost of the business, updated regularly to reflect profits and salaries paid. While many companies show goodwill in their balance sheet, the majority don't know how to show brand equity, or how to calculate it.

The first evidence of brand equity being reported to shareholders as part of a company's financial report was in the late 1980s, in the United Kingdom, when Nestle entered their acquisition of Rowntree on its balance sheet. Other companies followed suit, but the real breakthrough occurred when one of the UK's best known companies defended a hostile takeover by calculating the value of their brands and including them as an asset in the business. With one entry in the ledger, the company dramatically increased the price of the takeover and defeated the hostile bid.

Interestingly, it was the accounting and finance professions in Australia, the UK and New Zealand, rather than the US, that were the first to make provision for brands to be recognised as assets. That was in 1999. More than a decade later it is still not common practice, and for all our growing sophistication, the potential power of brands is a largely misunderstood concept, too narrowly defined by most to fully exploit its potential.

From a financial perspective, brand equity is acknowledged as the basis for an attractive long-term investment. Companies pay inflated prices for a brand because it is often cheaper than the cost of creating a new brand from scratch, although the process to do so is relatively straightforward.

Take a name like Di Bella Coffee, create a level of awareness around the name, synonymous with the promise of the ultimate coffee experience so that every time someone sees the Di Bella logo that expectation is their one and only thought. Commit to delivering a level of quality that is consistent with the promise, while building around it a set of associations that consistently reinforce the promise, and, finally, make sure you protect your asset. The end result, if you get it right, should be brand loyalty, which can then be converted into brand equity.

Sounds easy, simple and straightforward, I can hear you say, or perhaps not, perhaps you're having second thoughts.

To make more sense of it, maybe a short history lesson would be worthwhile to understand how brand equity has evolved.

***

Brand comes from an Old Norse word *brandr* meaning to burn. The original designation of the term 'brand' was a name or a symbol burnt into the hide of an animal or the side of a barrel. Whiskey distillers in Scotland, breweries in the UK and cattle ranchers in the US were amongst the first producers to use the idea of a brand to either protect their property or to differentiate their product from competitors. By the time the industrial revolution came along, this small group of early adopters was rapidly expanding. Hundreds of factories were belching out thick, black smoke from their chimneys and a never ending stream of products through the factory doors. All of these new products needed to find a market, so as competition increased and more and more mass produced commodities became available, pressure grew on manufacturers to find some way to mark, or brand, their goods.

At the outset, the new manufactured goods competed against traditional products that had satisfied people's needs for centuries. Communities had been largely self-sufficient in food and people rarely needed to travel too far afield to get what else they needed. Essential items of clothing, cooking implements, farm implements, building materials, even basics such as soap, were all produced locally.

The townspeople and the villagers trusted what they had and what they purchased. They knew the people who actually produced the goods and were loyal to traders who had served them for their entire lives. These same traders had extended credit to them, and in all probability were godparents to their children. In this environment loyalty was the linchpin.

Against this backdrop, 19th century mass producers were faced with the difficult task of persuading people to break their long-held habits and their long-serving loyalty to buy the new mass produced goods. To shift the huge volumes being made, manufacturers needed to be able to persuade people that they could trust the new product and that there were very good reasons why they should buy one manufacturer's product over another.

Initially, mass producers needed to create awareness of their products. Names we are familiar with today, including Ivory Soap, Sunlight, Campbell Soups, Kellogg's, Uncle Ben's, Quaker Oats and, of course, Coca-Cola, began to emerge. In the 1890s these were not the household names they are today but were new wave companies fighting tooth and nail with their competitors for every toe-hold in the market. *Marketing 101* or *Marketing for Dummies* would have been best-sellers had either existed. Branding as an idea was finally coming out of the closet, but it was still a relatively narrow concept aimed at building familiarity with the product.

*** 

A growing appreciation of the potential power of advertising to build awareness was the next step in the evolution of brand equity. The first newsprint advertisements appeared in England in the 18th century as printing and publishing costs became more affordable and people were hungry for news and information.

In its earliest guise, advertising was less about persuasion and more about information or communication. The role of advertising was to drive sales of new products in existing or new markets to encourage people to trial anything and everything. What advertising lacked in sophistication it made up for in enthusiasm.

Newspaper proprietors and salespeople knocked on doors, selling advertising space direct to anyone they considered to be a potential advertiser. Local store owners created their own advertisements, sometimes asking a friend who had studied literature at college, or a niece or nephew who had some artistic talent, to help.

In the second half of the 19th century, a US space broker, a person responsible for selling advertising space on behalf of the newspapers, saw an opportunity to set up the first advertising agency, offering the complete service of layout, copy and artwork. It didn't take long for mass producers to get on board, employing the emerging ad agencies to develop slogans and logos to differentiate their products. But security and prosperity for all of them was still in the awareness phase.

As the economies of nations expanded, the appreciation of the power of advertising grew exponentially. Against this backdrop, Lord Leverhulme, the founder of Lever Brothers, later to become half of the giant multinational Unilever, uttered his famous quote: "I know half my advertising isn't working, I just don't know which half."

The fact that advertising lacked any real sophistication in the early part of the 20th century shouldn't be surprising. The mass producers still believed they were selling commodities and were only interested in reaching as many prospective customers as they could. It's hard to say when the transition occurred, or whether these mass producers understood what was occurring, but at some point their commodities morphed into consumer goods, giving the 'Cinderella' brands their next massive step towards maturity by introducing the world to the concept of brand loyalty.

Loyalty hadn't died; it had just been forgotten. For decades, trial and expansion had dictated the ad spend of the mass producers. Tangible evidence was now emerging of repeat purchase and customer referral, and the more astute amongst the mass producers realised that advertising could play a key role in building loyalty to increase sales.

Mass production was an impatient master. New production techniques were making it possible to produce goods faster and faster. The cigarette business took on a whole new dimension when the automatic cigarette rolling machine was invented. The production of more and more cigarettes meant more and more markets needed to be opened, and more and more customers needed to be seduced into remaining loyal to their brand.

Fortunately, not all mass produced products were destined to become villains. People were getting used to the idea of new products that made their lives more comfortable and enjoyable. The end of World War II brought about a dramatic rise in consumerism. Families were taking advantage of a strengthening Western economy, filling their homes with refrigerators, washing machines, vacuum cleaners and other products designed to make their lives easier.

Subconsciously, consumers were getting used to the idea that there was competition for their favours. Advertisements urged them to try newer and more exciting, or more effective, products. In this environment, brands were proliferating, and it was largely due to the work of people like Lord Leverhulme setting the pace.

Lord Leverhulme, born William Lever, was not only famous for clever quotes; he was also a visionary and successful entrepreneur. He established Lever Brothers with his brother James in 1885. Partnering with a chemist from their home town, the brothers developed a new way of producing soap using palm oil and glycerine rather than tallow. The company went on to become Britain's first modern multinational.

Within a decade, Lever Brothers had launched three different brands of soap. The first, Sunlight, a free-lathering soap, was distributed to 134 countries. Lux and Lifebuoy weren't far behind, with Lever correctly predicting that customers would be prepared to indulge themselves if they could. Today, we take for granted the fact that a supermarket can carry twenty different soap brands on their shelves or that we can be confronted with just as many shower gels or liquid soaps. But, that hasn't always been the case.

Despite some amazing marketing breakthroughs, Lord Leverhulme was still one of a rare breed. While he capitalised on the willingness of customers to embrace the idea of brands, many more companies were still content to throw large parts of their profits at opening up new markets to expand consumption of their commodities. Most of these old-school mass producers weren't even aware that slowly but surely they were actually losing control. Only the canny and the resourceful, like Leverhulme, understood that the future of marketing, the future of brands, belonged to the customer, not to the mass producer.

With each passing decade intelligent entrepreneurs were able to reduce the percentage they wasted on advertising, advertising agencies were working hard on techniques to change attitudes and to find better ways to persuade customers to buy. They weren't always praised for their efforts. In the late 1950s Vance Packard attacked the exponents of advertising in his book *The Hidden Persuaders*. Packard claimed they were using psychology to get inside the heads of customers and consumers in what he described as a devious attempt to understand their motivations and trigger points to sell them goods they didn't need.

The potential power of brands was becoming evident to thinkers and strategists. A small but growing number of astute brand strategists were developing the very tools that Packard lambasted. They were never going to admit to it, but in their heart of hearts they knew that Vance Packard was very close to the money. Confident that most of their competitors continued to see the solution in simplistic terms, this small group of switched on strategists watched with a mixture of bemusement and amusement as the majority of manufacturers and business owners continued to ignore the revolution going on right under their noses.

And so the march to brand equity continued. One of the most savvy marketers and brand strategists of the 50s and 60s was an Englishman living in New York, the founder of the famous Ogilvy & Mather advertising agency. David Ogilvy was one of advertising's greatest copywriters. His book *Confessions of an Advertising Man* can still be found, and should be a must read for anyone wanting to understand the principles of great advertising. Ogilvy's campaigns were distinctive and timeless; more importantly, his copy sought out the emotional reason behind purchase decisions, and he mercilessly pursued it. His insight into the power of brands was compelling. He became one of the first to acknowledge the complexity of a brand, defining it as "an intangible sum of a product's attributes, its name, packaging, and price, its history, reputation, and the way it is advertised."

Finally, people in the know were articulating not only a definition for brand but were also capturing the concept of brand equity that today translates into US$98 billion of intangible brand value for Apple and US$93 billion of intangible brand value for Google.

If you are still asking why this is so important from an entrepreneurial intelligence perspective, let me put it into context. When customers pay little or no attention to brand in the purchase decision they are demonstrating no brand loyalty and the product or service has zero brand equity. At the other end of the scale, when customers continue to purchase a brand after a change has occurred – such as competitors dropping their price, or adding value to their offering, or even adding a feature to their product that makes it significantly more attractive or functional – then substantial brand equity is driving that level of loyalty.

In a nutshell, the evolution of brand equity underpinned the shift from product focus to customer focus. You couldn't look back and say, "There! That's the date it happened, that's when smart companies realised they needed to shift their focus from product to customer." As the history lesson of this chapter shows, the change was a gradual transition over several decades, but it was a profound change, and it is what we believe makes brands so unique and so powerful. This is the change that brought brand equity into sharp focus, and why the customer, in becoming pivotal to the power of brands, also became the single largest factor in calculating brand equity.

Perhaps the last word on the evolution of brands should be taken from a famous interview featured in the *Journal of Advertising Research* in the US. The person being interviewed is Larry Light, currently Global Chief Brands Officer for Intercontinental Hotels Group, the man acknowledged for turning around the marketing fortunes of McDonalds during the early part of this decade. In the interview, in the late 90s, Light was asked to paint a picture of marketing in the future:

> "The marketing battle will be a battle of brands, a competition for brand dominance. Businesses and investors will recognise brands as the company's most valuable assets. This is a critical concept. It is a vision about how to develop, strengthen, defend and manage a business … It will be more important to own markets than to own factories. The only way to own markets is to own market dominant brands."

And to own market dominant brands means that you must understand the role of the customer.

# 13

## Wanting people to come back

In Phillip Di Bella's business, there is only one imperative – delivering customer satisfaction. Do that well and you drive customer loyalty, customer referral and repeat business, which are the hallmarks of the coffee business, because they all hinge on one thing – satisfied customers. Not surprisingly they are also the benchmarks of every powerful brand. Think: Nike; think: McDonalds; think: Apple; think: Virgin; think: Microsoft. Is it any wonder that all the intelligent entrepreneurs we have discussed in this book demonstrate an intuitive grasp and understanding of the power of their brands?

Richard Branson showed an entrepreneur's intuitive understanding when he said, "The music industry is a strange combination of having real and intangible assets: pop bands are brand names in themselves, and at a given stage in their careers their name alone can practically guarantee hit records."

Of course they can, fifty years after their first British hit The Beatles are still selling more music every year than most of the contemporary artists who are considered to be commercially viable.

Consider your own experience with brands. In a previous chapter we asked you to look around your home, or your office; to look inside your wardrobe and on your shelves. Do the shirts hanging in the wardrobe all have a polo player motif on the chest, or do the fashion accessories in your drawer feature the famous double Gs?

Are you a loyal customer to a number of brands, in a number of different product categories? Do you always use the same brand of toothpaste or the same box of tissues? What about the perfume on your dresser or the training shoes in your gym bag – always the same?

Then ask yourself the question why? More to the point, ask yourself what is the relationship you have with that particular brand?

Because that's what brands do – they build relationships based on loyalty. The success of any brand is in the relationship between the consumer and the product or service for sale. Strong relationships are the very cornerstone of success for any business, because they represent repeat business.

The power of brands to create loyal customers, repeat business and referrals lies in *wanting* people to come back, not them *having to* come back. This is not a one-dimensional concept, nor is it one that has the same exact formula for always getting it right, but there are two aspects of powerful brands that will determine whether people want to come back, two things that you must get right to have any hope of that happening. Neither is earth shattering, nor out of reach for anyone.

If you want people to people to come back; firstly, you must understand every single aspect of your brand, both the tangible and the intangible aspects that impact on your customers. It's no good just understanding the tangible reasons; you must also understand what the intangible, emotional connections are as well. Once you understand them, the second part should come easily. Once you understand what your customers want, then you have to determine how you can manage and control every part of your brand so that the customer experience is always consistent.

Think of the brands you have a relationship with. Take one

of them and ask yourself this question: is the value of this brand greater or lesser than the tangible asset? Let's imagine for a moment that the product you have in your hand is a mobile phone. I'm assuming that it's your phone, not someone else's. Consider the tangible reasons why you chose that particular phone. Next, consider the intangible reasons, things that you can't immediately put your finger on.

So, how did you go? Did you finish up with a list of tangible reasons? Yes? Of course you did. How about intangibles? Not quite so sure, or are you? If you've got a list of both, then ask yourself this: which played the more decisive role in your decision to buy that phone – the tangible or the intangible. (Don't forget, the only person who loses if you cheat on the answer is you!)

People perceive the value of a branded product or service to be greater than the sum of its tangible assets. Many of the intangibles are difficult to pinpoint. Often they are individual and personal to each consumer. Unfortunately, the onus is on the person building the brand – the intelligent entrepreneur – to be as clear and definitive as they can.

Some of the tangible reasons that may make you want to return are relatively straight forward: convenient location, the only service in town, the colour matches your eyes. Once upon a time petrol companies such as Shell, BP, or going back in time, Golden Fleece and Amoco, actively portrayed the tangible benefits of buying your fuel at their outlets – none of this 'fill it yourself' business; instead, smartly dressed attendants filled your tank for you. Of course loyalty to petrol companies has diminished dramatically over the decades, replaced by a discounting mentality that overrides everything. Today, the tangible strength of these companies exists in the lure of a sign out the front which screams 4 CENTS OFF.

A significant and tangible part of the strength of supermarket brands is in their location. The major supermarket chains spend significant sums with demographers and town planners to understand where population shifts are occurring so that they can strategically plan expansion based on location, location, location. Then they spend another fortune on rents at the major shopping centres to make sure you can't avoid them.

These are tangible, inescapable parts of the supermarket brand offering. The intangibles are not as clear cut and perhaps not so compelling in the eyes of many.

For the better part of thirty years, Woolworths, in Australia, has built a brand reputation as the "Fresh Food People". The strategic premise was simple: offer a perceived point of difference that their major competitor can't, or wouldn't, match.

The rationale was also simple. Sales in supermarkets are broken down into dry groceries (what is stacked in all of the aisles), frozen foods and fresh foods. Although the figures are loose, let's round them out and say that the breakdown is one-third, one-third, one-third.

Woolworths strategized that there wasn't much of a point of difference in dry groceries or frozen foods. Most supermarkets stock the same brands and offer similar pricing. Where they did see an edge was in fresh foods: fresh fruit, fresh vegetables, fresh meat and fresh fish. Even fresh salads and other products that required a level of value adding but still met the definition of fresh.

Woolworths focused on revitalising this aspect of their business. Presentation was critical, so was delivering on the promise of 'fresh'. For three decades, Woolworths dominated the supermarket scene.

Today the picture is different. Coles supermarkets are in the ascendancy. Sales have lifted dramatically. The Coles presence in the market is much more visible, thanks to smart promotion and sponsorships. The store presentation is more vibrant, more alive. But is it only clever advertising or a lick of paint that has made the difference? Of course, the answer is no. Much of the answer lies in the intangibles, even, perhaps, in the intangibles associated with the Woolworth's brand.

Why donate to one charity over another? Most people donate

because they believe the charity can do some good, can make a difference. Or there is a personal association. We all know someone who has had cancer. If they die, next time we are asked to donate, we open our wallets and purses without hesitation. Great brands understand this kind of intangible and use it as a key part of their strategy.

The emotional response is a minefield for service organisations. One of the major Australian banks acknowledged that the customer experience had become jaded and that they, the banks, were responsible for it being allowed to occur. To counter this trend, NAB launched a campaign announcing they were 'breaking up' with the other banks. In a practical sense the announcement was supported by a move to reduce, or eliminate, banking fees, which were seen by customers as onerous and just profit-making. On an emotional level, the campaign sought to persuade customers that by breaking up with the other banks they were deliberately ending their involvement in bad banking relationships and would thereby become unpopular with the other banks. Clever strategy, but the proof, as always, will be in the number of new customers the bank gains and the numbers of old customers it retains.

Communications, in particular its delivery, has become an essential part of our existence. More than four billion mobile phone subscribers walk the earth. No doubt there is a mobile phone within a metre radius of where you are at the moment. Forget the phone for the moment; this is not about which smart phone brand you prefer but about who you use to provide your service. What made you choose that particular telco? Price, reliability, the package or perhaps it was the coverage offered? Or is it a complicated mix of all the above? When was the last time you changed providers, and why?

Nine times out of ten the reason to move on will be an emotional reason; only occasionally will it be a practical one. Perhaps someone failed to deliver on a promise; perhaps the time you spent waiting for a customer service operator to provide you with information was too long; or, worse still, they failed to give you an answer. We wonder how many people have changed telcos because they were angry and emotional about something.

Wanting customers to return and understanding the tangibles and intangibles is at the heart of Phillip Di Bella's vision of the ultimate coffee experience.

"Our goal from day one was to give the customers a memorable coffee experience, to make sure they wanted to return. We started by developing a selection of signature blends to suit any coffee palate. To make that happen we had to be able to control the tangible strengths of our brand. So, from the very start, we purchased only the highest quality beans, from the world's finest coffee growing regions. We identified the characteristic flavour unique to that area. Then we blended and freshly roasted these premium-grade beans to reach their optimum flavour and aroma at our own roasting warehouses around Australia."

Think about the implication of Phillip's comments in terms of tangible benefits, where brand equity is regarded as the sum total of the customer's experience. This is not about luck, or being in the right place at the right time; this is a set of conscious decisions and investments made by Phillip Di Bella to ensure customers are able to enjoy the ultimate coffee experience. In this instance, it starts with the development of a purchasing policy, the function of which is grounded in the knowledge and capacity to identify quality. On Phillip's part, that's a major investment in the right people with the requisite skills to know what they are doing; people with the necessary experience and confidence to criss-cross the globe looking for the right product.

Blending and roasting also require a significant investment in equipment, know-how and experience to deliver the optimum flavour and aroma. Phillip is a master; he has spent many years fine-tuning his skills to blend the beans to achieve a consistency of flavour. He makes sure his skills are shared with his people so they learn the same art. An approach to quality control, known as 'cupping', is fastidiously observed to evaluate the aroma and flavour profile of a blend. Then there is the equipment Phillip uses. All of Di Bella Coffee's roasting equipment is manufactured in Italy, to Phillip's specifications, to ensure it will deliver the specific flavour and aroma profiles that make Di Bella Coffee unique.

These investments are significant parts of the customer experience. Some are tangible assets, shown as such on the balance sheet. Some of them are less tangible and, as such, need to be acknowledged by the accountants and investment firms when calculating the brand equity that is at the heart of Interbrand's Top 100 ranking. These calculations acknowledge that a strong brand drives the bottom line by influencing customer choice and engendering loyalty. But the implications of brand equity go way beyond that.

This is where the intangible intersects with the tangible; where the emotional, not reasons grounded in fact, start to influence the customer's decision to come back. Unfortunately, these things never need happen.

Phillip Di Bella recognises that he and his organisation are not just dealing with a physical connection. He understands that there is a massive emotional connection between the brand and the consumer, and that it is sometimes very difficult to get a handle on an intangible such as an emotion.

The very foundation of Di Bella Coffee's brand is a powerful relationship with their customers that makes them want to come back again and again and again. Any business can do it; every business can build a successful brand, but only if the managers are empowered to put their brand at the centre, at the very heart, of their business strategy.

How you build loyalty, the investment made in ensuring your customers come back, is a complex set of deliverables, not a one-dimensional easy fix. Product development, staff development and the marketing and advertising investment are all part of building brand loyalty and, ultimately, the value or equity in your brand. Every part of the operation has the potential to build or knock down the brand promise.

A batch of burnt roasted beans, not fully destroyed, find their way into a customer's order – the mistake could occur through carelessness, or by accident – and the end result is a disgruntled café owner who returns the offending package directly to Phillip's office. The café owner is rightfully angry, his customers are his lifeblood. The phone conversation is painful because Phillip has taken every step to train and educate his people on the power of the brand and the need to deliver on the brand's relationship with their customers. It happens. The lesson is to make sure it doesn't happen ever again. Phillip moves quickly to identify where the error occurred, whether it was human mistake or mechanical failure, and takes the steps necessary to eliminate the problem.

Ironically, this breakdown highlights how far-reaching the power of a strong brand can be. The strength of the Di Bella Coffee brand actually increases Phillip Di Bella's chances of securing the right people to work for him, and to retain the valuable employees he wants to retain. One of the strengths underpinning Di Bella Coffee's brand strategy is to be an 'employer of choice'. The fundamental premise behind the goal is that employee satisfaction is paramount to the success of the organisation. Satisfaction is in part resolved by sharing the wealth that is generated; however, far more important drivers of satisfaction and retention are strategies around working conditions, career paths and continual learning. The HR exponents will tell you that these factors are often given greater credence by employees in satisfaction rankings than is the size of their pay-packet.

The lesson to take away is very simple: Your brand must become the relationship between the customer and the product or service you are offering. The strength of that relationship is simply measured by the loyalty shown in repeat purchase.

The ultimate aim of branding is to manage the image of a product or service in such a way that it creates an identity that consumers want to relate to and, in turn, continue to purchase. A great brand only exists because of the strength of response by the consumer to its promise. The people who create great brands know that their wealth is in that same response, and that they can only protect that wealth while they continue to deliver what the consumer wants in a consistent manner. And sometimes that isn't as easy as it looks.

Managing the image of a product or service so that it creates a desirable identity, which is greater than the sum of its parts, is Phillip Di Bella's conscious and unconscious goal every day. His aim is to create a brand that, first and foremost, meets the customer's expectation of 'What's in it for me?', a brand that the consumer can relate to, and, lastly, but most importantly, a brand the customer will want to keep buying.

One sobering note before we close this chapter.

Perhaps the most important thing to understand about your brand, something that may come as a shock after investing a great deal of effort and money into building your brand, is this: While you may control your brand, while you may be the one driving your brand, you don't own the brand. You can never own the brand, because the customer owns it.

Phillip Di Bella acknowledges this as one of the most difficult ideas people need to get their heads around in understanding the power of a brand.

"The customer owns the brand because they are the ones who put their hand in their pocket to make the purchase. It really is that simple. Every one of the brands mentioned in this book depends on the customer putting their hand in their pocket to purchase product. The reason they will keep putting their hands in their pockets is out of loyalty to the brand, but loyalty can be as fragile as their last experience."

But don't be despondent. By understanding that the customer owns the brand we can then define brand equity as simply the sum total of the assets and liabilities linked to the brand that either add value to, or take value away from, the customer experience. In the case of the Di Bella Coffee brand, the customer experience is securely in Phillip's control.

# 14

## Telling a story so compelling

"Telling a story so compelling it inspires people to choose your product" is how Phillip Di Bella defines marketing. It's a very insightful description because it focuses the function of marketing right where it should be, on the needs of the customer. Like Branson and Jobs, and 99% of the world's successful entrepreneurs, Phillip Di Bella understands that customer needs are at the heart of powerful brands, and that marketing is essentially the art of brand building.

In the chapter on brand equity we lamented the failure of most 20th century mass producers to embrace the concept of brand. In doing so they also failed to understand the function of marketing. Marketing is a broad canvas; it is also the victim of too many text books written in dry, unemotional and uninspiring language. Some people treat the four Ps of product, price, place (distribution) and promotion as having mystical qualities. Others treat them with a degree of derision, quick to joke when a fifth or even sixth P is added by someone wanting to add clarity, rather than providing material for someone's stand-up routine. Unfortunately, ignorance about marketing isn't only confined to the mass producers of the past.

As we move further into the 21st century, marketing is still viewed by many business owners and so-called entrepreneurs as a narrow concept. I hate to think how many times I have been handed a business card with the job description Sales and Marketing Manager. Any half-awake marketing student will tell you that the principles of marketing swing into action long before you even have a product to sell. All too often CEOs relegate marketing to a function within a department that doesn't have the authority to really drive results. Others define the function incorrectly, referring to a communications role, as in "my marketing department."

These types of mistakes and narrow minded thinking are not the hallmarks of intelligent entrepreneurs like Phillip Di Bella, whose definition of marketing puts him in the same camp as Peter Drucker. Drucker once observed that "the aim of marketing is to make selling superfluous." The only way that selling can become superfluous is when a brand understands its customer needs completely and prepares and packages it in such a way that people will be compelled to buy; two different takes on the same subject, one a successful entrepreneur, the other a world renowned business commentator, both pointing you in the same direction. Get the basics right and selling becomes unnecessary, thanks to the unmitigated power of your brand.

The success of every brand, including yours, is locked inextricably to your customer's perceptions about what you offer, and your ability to deliver on their expectations. Your brand is the sum total of what your customers think about your service or your product. Which means the starting point for any powerful brand must come from an understanding of the customer's WiiFM, or What's in it for me? More to the point, understanding your customer's WiiFM means that you need to look at your business from a customer's point of view. But first, you need to be very clear in your own mind about what business you are in.

In 1960, when Theodore Levitt introduced the phrase 'marketing myopia', in an article for the *Harvard Business Review*, it was seen by the more astute business thinkers as a turning point in marketing thinking. Their hope was that it would be a significant nail in the coffin of the mass producers by shifting the emphasis, once and for all, away from the product and onto the customer.

In his article, Levitt argued that that there was no such thing as a growth industry, but, rather, that every major industry had once been a growth industry and had either stopped growing or was in decline. At the heart of Levitt's claim was a fact so depressingly simple it should have sent shivers up the spine of America's top industrialists. Levitt argued that industry growth slowed or stopped, not because the market was saturated, as the so-called experts postulated, but because management had become so obsessed with their product that they completely ignored their customers' needs. To prove his argument he identified an embarrassingly increasing number of industries and companies that were defining their business so narrowly that they were unable to take advantage of growth or change.

As discussed in Chapter 5, the first industry he pointed to was the US railways, which had stopped growing and was in serious financial trouble, contending that they didn't stop growing because passenger needs and freight transportation had declined. In fact, in America in the 50s and 60s, transportation needs were growing exponentially. This was a period of significant growth for much of the Western world following the end of World War II. New industries were emerging, consumerism was on a rapidly ascending curve and people were open to new ideas and new ways of doing things. The demise of the US railways was not a case of the need for transport declining, Levitt argued, but because they allowed other modes of transport to take customers away from them.

Instead of acting on their customers' needs and desires, which were changing, the management of the American railways clung to the presumed longevity of their products, defining their industry narrowly as railway oriented instead of transport oriented. Instead of filling their customers' changing needs, they sat back while different transport solutions came and took their customers away. Where once customers accepted that the end of the line meant just that the end of the rail line, service savvy customers of the 1960s were expecting more for their loyalty, and they were getting it.

From the American railways, Levitt then took aim at Hollywood. The movie industry was in serious trouble. Many of the major studios, and the movie moguls who controlled them, were threatened with extinction. For several decades, television had been making inroads into the world of entertainment, but it would be too simplistic to point the finger at television as the reason for the demise of movie industry. No, Levitt argued, it wasn't television but the movie moguls own myopia that had forced so many of them into drastic reorganisation. The moguls, he contended, defined their business incorrectly. They thought they were in the movie business when they should have been thinking of themselves as part of the entertainment business, with the myriad of options that were tempting the customer's discretionary dollar.

In an age when Australia was described as riding on the sheep's back, the dry cleaning industry could have been forgiven for believing its future was rosy. In fact, Levitt argued, the industry was on the verge of obsolescence due to the growth of synthetic fabrics and non-iron fabrics.

Some people were either listening to Levitt or were staking out their own claims to a similar philosophy. One such man in the 60s was Robert Townsend, the newly appointed CEO of Avis Car Rentals. Avis had been losing money for the better part of a decade. When Townsend came on board he suspected that the culture and the focus of the company were wrong. What happened next was a massive leap forward for marketing and mankind.

Townsend argued to his board and to his senior management team that the company was NOT in the car rental business, but, rather, Avis was in the used car business. Confronting his bewildered management team, Townsend asked them to identify the primary waste product of the car rental business. No prizes if you correctly answered cars. In fact, Avis created enough waste product to make the company the world's second largest producer of used cars. No prizes, either, for guessing who was the number one producer of used cars. A hint, the company in question is the primary reason why Avis introduced the positioning line "We try harder".

By defining the business of Avis as used cars, Townsend was putting himself squarely and effectively inside the minds of his customers. What Townsend had recognised was that the customer experience for anyone renting an Avis car was not all that great. Admittedly it wasn't that much inferior to the experience people received from Avis's competitors, but it was enough of a difference.

The culture at Avis was about getting the maximum return from each vehicle. Fair enough, except that such a culture is likely to produce a mind-set of budget savings and perhaps even cutting corners. Perhaps the cars weren't always serviced as often as they should be; perhaps the cars weren't washed between each hiring; perhaps customers were allowed to smoke in an Avis rental car, leaving it somewhat unpleasant for the senses of the next hirer; or perhaps the cars were allowed to rack up more miles, or kilometres, than was optimal for their re-sale value.

Perhaps!

What is undeniable is that if you approached the business with a used car mind-set then you approached each of those customer disincentives from a completely different perspective. First, your objective in the used car business doesn't change – you still want to get the maximum return on your dollar investment. Only this time your return depends on how well you have protected your asset rather than on how much you have been able to extract from it.

To maximise the sale price and return of your used car it makes sense to have it serviced regularly, and thoroughly. It makes sense to clean it after every hiring, and to even place a small rubbish bag in the car for people to use. It makes sense to place a limit on the number of miles or kilometres each vehicle can run up, and it makes sense to ban smoking from your vehicles.

As I said, Townsend put himself inside the minds of his hire customers and he came up with a customer experience that was second to none. He also came up with a lucrative income stream for his company, in the used car business, which saw Avis trading in the black after his first year at the helm.

Unfortunately, the record shows that over the past fifty years supposedly smart and astute managers have not been listening. In the same way mass producers buried their heads in the sand in the 1920s and 30s, many companies have foundered through the second half of the 20th and the beginning of the 21st centuries by disregarding Levitt's warning and not heeding the lessons of people like Robert Townsend. The most depressing case of recent times where a company has not defined its business well has been the decline and liquidation of Kodak. Kodak persisted well beyond the point of becoming terminal, believing its future was in the film business rather than the digital business. What must be even more galling for the remaining fans of Kodak is the realisation that Kodak actually invented the digital camera, only to leave its development well down the list of company priorities.

As Theodore Levitt pointed out so adroitly fifty years earlier, products and markets change! To be an intelligent and successful entrepreneur means you not only need to embrace change, you need to be vigilant about it.

# 15

## Brand DNA

Ever heard the term deoxyribonucleic acid? Does it help if I tell you that the scientific definition of deoxyribonucleic acid is the molecule that encodes the genetic instructions used in the development and functioning of all known living organisms and many viruses? Still none the wiser? Don't worry; you're not on your own.

However, it'd be nigh on impossible to find someone who hasn't heard the acronym that defines deoxyribonucleic acid: DNA.

DNA has infiltrated every corner of the globe through millions of copies of hugely successful novels by authors such as Patricia Cornwell, Karin Slaughter and Kathy Reichs. The irony is that the books, like the hundreds of television programs that also deal with forensic science, and the thousands of scripts Hollywood, Bollywood and every other film industry reviews each year on the subject, all mirror the real life implications of DNA. In every book and every screenplay, the plot lines are impressively similar. The ability of the writers to cut and paste dialogue from a character in one program to a character of different sex in another program is just like solving the intricacies of DNA that the stories portray. It's like building with Lego; all the parts link together in an amazingly intricate and surprisingly similar way, enabling different variations on a theme to be released year after year.

Just like human DNA.

A brand's DNA is really no different. Your brand's DNA may well comprise the same pieces of DNA as those used by one of your competitors. These are the fundamental parts of the DNA chain, the basic building blocks required to get started. In the case of a coffee company like Di Bella Coffee the brand DNA connects coffee beans with roasting equipment, and then links the product with packaging and a network of distribution.

The difference between your brand and that of your competitors is exactly the same as two children who use the same pieces of Lego to build different outcomes. Success lies in how you put the parts of the puzzle together. Building your brand is about selecting the right parts and putting them together in such a way that they respond to the needs of your customers.

So, how do you define the brand DNA of your business?

The answer is linked to the same kind of process scientists use to examine human DNA, but in reverse. DNA profiling of humans enables forensic scientists to determine the identity of the person who committed the crime through the uniqueness of their DNA. A person's DNA is what makes them unique. What Phillip Di Bella set out to understand through an analysis of his business were the values that would make his brand unique in the minds of his customers, and set it apart from his competitors.

For Di Bella Coffee, the brand DNA starts in Brazil, New Guinea or parts of Africa, or one of thirteen other countries they import from, to ensure they have the right beans for the right blend. It is then linked to the finest Italian coffee making equipment to roast the beans to perfection. Quality packaging sourced from China is then connected to fresh seal technology from Australia. The links in the brand DNA chain continue, with Mercedes vans painted in black, gold and white livery delivering freshly roasted beans to café owners across the country. The brand DNA then connects through market development executives who travel the length and breadth of the land helping start-up businesses learn about coffee: how to grind for optimum flavour; the art of the crema; what is too hot, what is too cold. The chain then engages with formal workforce development plans, which identify product knowledge gaps so that training courses can be developed and implemented in the field.

Once you've identified all the parts, or links, of a brand's DNA, it is a straightforward task to determine a strategy based on the customer's perspective. The Di Bella brand strategy is a case in point. Nothing is done in the company unless it is measured against the customer's likely response. The Director of Corporate Services has in place a training program to ensure everyone in the organisation is customer-centric. Listen to the people taking orders over the phone: the relationship with the caller is warm and friendly, and, most importantly, they are able to anticipate the customer's needs because they know who the customer is, the coffee they order, their other needs, even so far as to alert them to the fact that Di Bella will be closed on the day of their next order due to a public holiday, so when would they like to receive their order. Attention to detail and the requisite product knowledge reinforce in the customer's mind Di Bella's vision of the ultimate coffee experience.

Don't be alarmed if the first question you are asked by someone who understands brand DNA is whether you are about drill bits or holes, or whether you want a vacuum cleaner or a clean house; a washing machine or clean clothes; a mobile phone or a chat with your mother. Customers don't buy the features of a product or service, they buy the anticipated outcome. In other words, customers don't buy the attributes; they buy the benefit – the benefit to them.

A home handyperson doesn't buy a drill bit because they want a shiny, long piece of metal. They buy the drill bit because they need to hang a picture on a wall or repair a piece of furniture that has a collapsed leg. A house-proud mum doesn't buy a vacuum cleaner to store in the linen closet, she buys a vacuum cleaner to make sure she can navigate around her young daughter's bedroom without standing in an inadvertent spill of sprinkles. It's the same with the washing machine and the mobile phone. Insurance companies don't sell policies, they sell peace of mind; tyre retailers don't sell rubber, they sell safety. The list is endless. Every product or service with a list of features or attributes as long as your arm ultimately needs to translate each one of those attributes into What's in it for me?

So your starting point to examine your brand's DNA is to understand the difference between attributes and benefits.

On a sheet of paper, draw a line vertically from the top of the page to the bottom. On the left side of the page, write Attributes as a heading. On the other side, write Benefits. Now begin to compile a list of the features or attributes of your business. They can be rational (tangible) or emotional (intangible). In the coffee business, the list might look something like this:

| ATTRIBUTES | BENEFITS (WiiFM) |
| --- | --- |
| Freshly roasted beans | |
| Genuine Italian designed and manufactured espresso machines | |
| Same day delivery | |
| Friendly, efficient service | |
| Exceptional product knowledge | |
| Vacuum packed and sealed | |
| Variety of blends | |
| As required stock holding | |
| All accessories available | |
| National presence | |
| Roasting warehouses | |

This list may not be exhaustive but it captures many of the distinctive attributes Phillip Di Bella analysed. Now we need to translate them into benefits. In this case, the WiiFM from the perspective of a café owner who is a customer of Di Bella Coffee.

| ATTRIBUTES | BENEFITS (WiiFM) |
|---|---|
| Freshly roasted beans | My customers love the amazing taste, the wonderful aroma |
| Genuine Italian designed and manufactured espresso machines | Traditional taste, true to the origins of great coffee |
| Same day delivery | Fresh coffee – you can smell the difference |
| Friendly, efficient service | I enjoy dealing with them - they make my life easy |
| Exceptional product knowledge | They add real value to my customers' experience |
| Vacuum packed and sealed | Fresh coffee that stays fresh |
| Variety of blends | I select the blend that best suits my customers |
| As required stock holding | Fresh coffee |
| All accessories available | One stop shop for my needs |
| National presence | Fresh, responsive |
| Roasting warehouses across the country | It's a very personal experience |

The fact that there is a level of repetition should be taken as a strength of the brand analysis, not a weakness. In fact, you can already get a sense of the emerging uniqueness of Di Bella's positioning, particularly when you relate these benefits to Phillip Di Bella's original vision – the ultimate coffee experience.

\*\*\*

The next part of establishing a brand's DNA is to understand the values of the brand, the principles held by the company or products that make you feel good about your association with them. When a hardware chain offers a guarantee that it will not be beaten on price, the intention is to reinforce your opinion that you can trust their claim, and therefore their brand. When a jewellery store offers to clean your jewellery, they are doing so in the expectation that they are not just interested in you when you buy something but are willing to invest in a much stronger relationship.

Phillip Di Bella began Di Bella Coffee with a strong sense of the values he intended to use to run the company. He called these values PACII, an acronym that stood for the five values he believed every single one of the people who worked for Di Bella Coffee should live by. These values are in many ways a statement about the sort of person Phillip Di Bella is, and the sort of brand he wanted to build. The first of those values was **Passion**.

"Passion is at the core of our business. There is a sense of passion from the top down, because we believe in not only in our products but our people as well. Skills can be taught, but an attitude is one of the most valuable attributes a staff member can offer our company.

The second PACII value Phillip insisted on when he established the company was **Accountability**, a trait that would be essential in every employee if Phillip was going to achieve his vision.

"I was determined to give everyone who worked at Di Bella Coffee job ownership so that, in turn, they had job purpose. From the very outset, staff and management were given clear expectations of what was expected of each other and the responsibility to make decisions and implement systems and procedures to help make them accountable for the decisions they made."

The third PACII value Phillip established for the company was **Consistency**, which, along with accountability, is vitally important if the brand promise of Di Bella Coffee is to be delivered.

"From the very beginning I was committed to achieving consistency, not only in our product but in our company. I wanted every part of Di Bella Coffee to be singing the same song. Communication was the key, so we established regular touch-points through team meetings and barista jams to ensure that the messages we were sending remained consistent."

The fourth value Phillip set in stone was **Inspiration**. This is an intriguing value from a brand perspective, but one that exemplifies the mantle of intelligent entrepreneurship. Inspiration is something that we normally associate with great sports stars or highly motivated and successful leaders, maybe even the odd politician or two. In Phillip's set of values, inspiration is a prerequisite of every employee, who he charges with inspiring themselves, each other and their clients about the brand.

"Di Bella Coffee is here to educate, not dictate. One of our company mantras is 'be better tomorrow than what we are today'. Management has always been encouraged to lead by example, and staff are encouraged to embark on not only a professional journey but a personal journey. If people are not inspired on a personal level, I don't believe they can inspire our customers. From the day we opened the doors, I have been determined to create an inspiring work environment where staff would be given the opportunity to think outside the square, a place with an open door policy and a continual learning environment for everyone."

The final PACII value is **Integrity**, and it is last for a very good reason. Consider what we have already said about the brand and the level of trust that is required to build loyalty. Honesty, principle and honour are the very foundations of that trust, and they are the core components of integrity.

"I have always believed you have to do the right thing by others. We always strive to do what is right for our customers, our staff and each other. We under-promise and over-deliver in terms of customer service, we have an open and transparent decision-making process, and we encourage accountability in our staff. We understand people make mistakes, however we strive to 'be better tomorrow than what we are today.'"

The PACII values that Phillip Di Bella established from the outset have evolved over time. They are reviewed constantly to ensure they are still relevant, and that they are being delivered.

\*\*\*

One final word, and perhaps a caution about setting values that the brand will be judged by.

Honesty and integrity are often cited as fundamental values by a range of companies, big and small. They set them as an integral part of their brand promise. However, these values can be double-edged swords. The Australian Heart Foundation promotes food products that have been identified as low in fats and sugars and therefore good for the heart. Such products are awarded the Heart Foundations tick of approval. A fee is payable to the Heart Foundation for the approved product, or organisation, to use in their marketing. It is a powerful endorsement to a nation that is still to fully acknowledge its obesity problem.

However, and here is the double-edged sword, the credibility of the Heart Foundation and their tick of approval took a pounding when they authorised McDonalds to use the tick on certain products. McDonalds deployed their latest marketing coup and were widely criticised in the media for appearing to apply the tick across a broader range of products than those that had been approved. The Heart Foundation was also vilified, not only for allowing McDonalds to damage the credibility of the tick, but for damaging the name of legitimate healthy products by associating the tick with McDonalds products.

The media, and other commentators, may not have had all the facts right but the subsequent loss of trust in the brand will cause the Heart Foundation to be particularly cautious in future.

***

The fourth part of a brand's DNA is its personality. We all have particular (some may say peculiar) personality traits that define us. It is no different for a brand. You will often find researchers asking respondents to identify the type of human personality characteristics a brand or product demonstrates. The same researchers have established frameworks to identify core dimensions of brand personality in order that there is consistency. One such framework was developed by Jennifer Aaker and reported in the *Journal of Market Research*.

In her model, Aaker identified sincerity, excitement, competence, sophistication and ruggedness as the key factors to describe an individual's behaviour and beliefs, while also capturing their physical and demographic characteristics. A sincere personality equated to honesty and authenticity; excitement incorporated traits of daring, spirit and imagination; a competent personality meant reliability, responsibility, dependability and efficiency; sophisticated personalities were seen as glamorous, perhaps at times pretentious, always charming and romantic; and rugged personalities were thought to be tough and strong, while spending a lot of time outdoors.[5]

The epitome of brand personality would have to be the Harley Davidson. Two American researchers,[6] themselves owners of Harleys, identified three core values that were shared by their fellow bikers. They were all seeking the personal freedom of riding a motorcycle, as opposed to the confines of a car. Patriotism was high on the list, and this was demonstrated over and over by the rejection of imported bikes – no self-respecting Harley rider would ever deign to lift a leg over a Japanese copy.

There was another value that was harder to pin down, a value inspired by the famous photo of Marlon Brando in the movie *Wild Ones*, decked out in leather cap, astride his Harley, riding towards the camera. It's hard to ignore the image this creates, or the personality of the brand as a macho, patriotic, freedom-seeking person at home on the road.

Phillip Di Bella might argue with me on this, but there is no doubt in my mind that using Aaker's model the brand personality for Di Bella Coffee must be a mix of sincerity, sophistication and competence. The vision of the ultimate coffee experience sits very comfortably with a personality that is at the same time glamorous, always charming and romantic, authentic, reliable and efficient.

*** 

5        Jennifer L. Aaker, "Dimensions of Brand Personality" *Journal of Marketing Research*, August 1997
6        John W. Schouten and James H. McAlexander, "Subcultures of Consumption: An Ethnography of the New Bikers," *Journal of Consumer Research* June 1995

A very powerful example of how these four parts of the brand DNA fit together comes from a woman who was no less than a Dame Commander of the British Empire.

Anita Roddick built a brand that brought her untold millions, the CBE, a wall full of awards for her environmental work and the thanks of thousands of people who she helped through charity work. Anita Roddick also gained her fair share of controversy before she died at the relatively young age of 64 from complications brought on from Hepatitis C.

Roddick was the founder of The Body Shop, an international chain of manufacturing and retail franchises of skin and hair care products. In Australia, The Body Shop is a wholly Australian owned company operating over 80 stores across the country. Anyone who has ever been inside one of the group's stores will know that The Body Shop only sells cosmetics made from natural ingredients. Roddick's intent was to appeal to people's concern for the environment rather than play to their vanity. Her approach was a long way from that espoused by Charles Revlon, who once said he didn't sell lipstick; he sold hope.

On her official website, Roddick tells the story of how The Body Shop came into being. She writes that she never expected to get rich from the venture, simply to survive. Of course she did survive, and her business flourished. The company began with one shop in Brighton, England, which Roddick established in 1976. She started with a small range of products made from natural ingredients, including honey, oats, seaweed, birch and cocoa. Everything was packaged in simple, recyclable containers, bereft of glitzy labelling.

Roddick's motivation was, in part, the privations of the World War II and the lessons she learnt from her mother, who wasted nothing and recycled everything she could for another use. The lesson was one adopted by Roddick, who began with the simple premise of reusing, refilling and recycling. Her belief in all things natural came from seeing first-hand the use of natural products to protect and nourish. Before marrying and starting her business, Anita Roddick had enjoyed an eclectic life, travelling the world, teaching at a kibbutz in Israel before moving on to spend time with farming and fishing communities in remote regions populated by pre-industrial peoples who depended on the land and the sea for their needs.

Much of her philosophy employed at The Body Shop emerged from these experiences. Her business skills were learnt on the go. She writes that the only business advice she ever received was from her husband, who advised her to ensure she took sales of £300 a week at the shop:

"Nobody talks of entrepreneurship as survival, but that's exactly what it is and what nurtures creative thinking. Running that first shop taught me business is not financial science, it's about trading: buying and selling. It's about creating a product or service so good that people will pay for it. Now, 30 years on, The Body Shop is a multi-local business with over 2,045 stores serving over 77 million customers in 51 different markets in 25 different languages across 12 time zones. And I haven't a clue how we got there."

It's somewhat disingenuous to suggest that she did not know how The Body Shop achieved its incredible success. Perhaps it would have been more appropriate, or more accurate, to acknowledge that her skills as an entrepreneur were intuitive, and right.

She painted her first shop green because it was the colour that best covered up the damp, mouldy walls. Fortuitously, or strategically, this was at a time when Europe and the rest of the world was beginning to understand the damage being done to the environment and the word green was being closely linked with the movement. Anita Roddick acknowledges that success is more than a good idea and that timing is a key part of success.

The decision to franchise the operation was a deliberate strategy to self-finance more stores. The idea was her husband's, but the basis for its immediate success was the brand's DNA.

The Body Shop happened at the right time and connected with all the right motivations, summed up best in the company's philosophy of "Profits with principle". Essentially, the world fell in love with Anita Roddick and The Body Shop because her customers wanted to do the right thing by the environment; they wanted to see organisations such as The Body Shop take a position where they could pursue social and environment change. Her customers applauded the fact that no animals were used to test their products, and they thumbed their noses at the unnecessary hype surrounding the rest of the cosmetic world.

Out with the fancy packaging and glamorous advertisements, and in with the frugal and the caring; in with social conscience and saving the rain forest and endangered animals, and in with feel-good factor and looking good naturally. If you ever wanted to see a brand that captures the essence of its customers' needs, look no further than The Body Shop.

The attributes were simple – natural ingredients from less industrialised countries. The benefits were enormous – more jobs to improve lives in poorer countries, along with a product perceived to be nutritious for your skin because it contained no chemicals.

The values were equally impressive, as summed up by the commitment given in the opening line of the company's mission statement: To dedicate our business to the pursuit of social and environmental change. Look at their website, of course you will find products, but you will also find the charities they support, causes they contribute to. The Body Shop values are flagged: against animal testing, support community fair trade, activate self-esteem, defend human rights, protect the planet. Why wouldn't customers want to be a part of that?

The personality comes through clearly: a caring, sharing organisation with a noble sense of purpose.

***

There is one final part of a brand's DNA, and it is probably the most difficult part to understand. It's what we will call the 'essence' of the brand, and it is a very complex fusion of the functional and emotional parts of the brand that bring the brand promise to life. This is the litmus test.

On their website, The Body Shop is defined as the original, ethical and natural beauty brand. But the essence of the brand for me is better summed up when they say, "Our values have always been at the heart of our business. In fact they're at the heart of everything we do – cosmetics with conscience."

Di Bella Coffee's brand is squarely focused on the customer. It is not a hyped up slogan like "Coke is it", or Nike's, "Just do it". Phillip Di Bella presents his brand as "the leading authority on specialty coffee from crop to cup". For Phillip, this is where the brand rubber hits the road, because failure to deliver on that promise means a failure to deliver the vision of the ultimate coffee experience

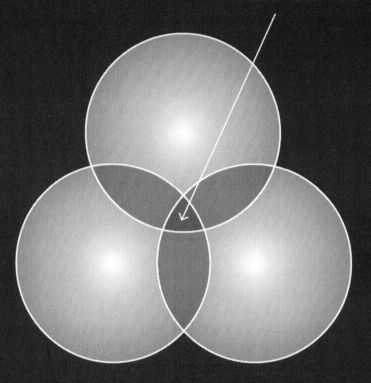

EMOTIONAL
INTELLIGENCE

# 16

# Intelligence isn't a number

I am sure most of my peers can recall a moment when a teacher, or someone who we looked up to, took us aside and bluntly told us we would never achieve our potential; that our grades were so average we would never make much of ourselves, and certainly never become great leaders. Because that teacher was in a position of presumed authority, we were unlikely to challenge their evaluation; in fact it is very hard for a young, impressionable person to challenge authority with conviction and insight. Of course the damage done was unimaginable, but, fortunately, a number of telling lessons emerged from such an inauspicious confrontation, all of them framed by a concept that is rapidly changing the world. It is a concept that is proving to be a significant leveller in business and politics, a concept that has been pivotal to the success of most of the great leaders and entrepreneurs of history, but which was only given a respectful title two decades ago.

I am talking about emotional intelligence, or EI.

Some people still dismiss the proposition of emotional intelligence out of hand.

Phillip Di Bella isn't one of them.

Phillip believes that emotional intelligence is a critical skill required by anyone who has ambitions to succeed. He enthusiastically agrees with the leading authorities on EI who argue that great leaders have a higher level of emotional intelligence than the average person. When I relate to him the experience so many people suffered at the hands of misguided authority figures, Phillip's response is unequivocal:

> "Everything I've learnt tells me that teacher got it fundamentally wrong. Not only wasn't the teacher showing any emotional intelligence in how they related to their students, but, more to the point, they obviously believed that the only measure of success is IQ; why else would they be so obsessed with the student's grades. That teacher failed to understand that a high level of EI is a much more powerful guide to who will, and who won't, be a powerful leader than the IQ measure they were probably evaluating. You can't ignore IQ, but to me everything revolves around emotional intelligence"

It probably comes as no surprise that I was one of those students. I still remember my penultimate year at secondary school when my history teacher took me aside and berated me for what I had thought was a well-prepared and well-structured essay on one of Australia's first, and possibly best known, entrepreneurs in the early history of Australia. Little did I realise that both the teacher and the story would come back to feature in this book.

As a 16-year-old, I was fascinated by the exploits of John Macarthur, the man famous for starting the Australian wool industry. As for the description of entrepreneur, I doubt my history teacher would have ever given that title to John Macarthur. Yet, anyone who has read the history of the man can't help but recognise the entrepreneurial skill he brought to all his ventures, in particular the enormous legacy he built for himself and his newly adopted country through the wool trade.

To many, he was a powerful leader; to others, including many historians, he was argumentative and headstrong. Although a serving officer in the NSW Corps, Macarthur appeared to dislike authority and caused the various Governors of the growing colony significant heartache. He argued with Governor Hunter, whom he alleged was trafficking in rum, and whom he also claimed was incompetent. Hunter ultimately returned to England, where he was forced to answer the charges of trafficking, a bonus to those in the colony who agreed with Macarthur about the Governor's competence.

Macarthur's relationship with Governor King, Hunter's successor, soured when King had Macarthur arrested for wounding a higher-ranked officer in a duel. The history books show that King later recanted and offered Macarthur the position of Commandant of Norfolk Island. Macarthur refused to accept the appointment, a resounding slap in the face for the new Governor, albeit one that went unpunished.

Following King's departure, Macarthur repeatedly clashed with new Governor Bligh, who believed the first priority for land use should be agriculture, not wool. Once again, John Macarthur's running battle with authority appeared to position him as the winner when he figured as a key player in the Rum Rebellion of 1808, when Governor Bligh was overthrown in a military coup.

So, was Macarthur a headstrong bully or a strong leader, an argumentative pain in the administration's side or a brilliant entrepreneur? Whichever way you want to call it, perhaps the proof lies in the first bale of Merino wool Macarthur sent to England. That bale of wool not only achieved a record price, it established, once and for all, the Merino brand on the international stage. The administration in the new NSW colony had tried to block Macarthur at every step. That it didn't succeed is testament to Macarthur's vision that would see wool play such a pivotal role in the economic future of Australia.

My ability to relate this piece of history has probably improved immeasurably from when I was sixteen, but I still felt enormously aggrieved that my earnest endeavours to capture the essence of one of Australia's first intelligent entrepreneurs was being rejected as a worthless piece of research, and was being used as the catalyst for an attack on my future worth as a human being.

I agree with Phillip Di Bella that my tyrannical history master showed a complete lack of emotional intelligence. Then again, this was at a time when EI was not at the forefront of curricula development. As Phillip pointed out, my history teacher was no doubt assessing me on my IQ rather than any understood notion of EI. He was assessing me against a required benchmark of grades that, without considering a high level of EI, is, at best, one-dimensional.

(Fortunately, my history teacher failed to achieve his objective and I went on to matriculate a year later with honours in history.)

Today, the notion of emotional intelligence surrounds us. It is present in every discussion we have, in every decision we take, in every instruction we give. It is present in the way we assess options, choose our friends or identify our enemies. Yet, for most of us, we don't wake up each morning and think about how we will apply emotional intelligence throughout the day. For that matter, most people probably don't wake up in the morning, get out of bed, stretch and then ask themselves how they will apply their IQ during the course of their day.

The application of knowledge is second nature to all of us. It is why we do what we do. Our IQ is a measurable test of our ability to complete tasks, but does it equip us to be better leaders, or better managers, or successful entrepreneurs? Of course the answer is not so equivocal.

Think about what you consider to be poor examples of leadership in the workplace. How many times has the situation been resolved by a manager exhibiting a higher IQ than the person being reprimanded?

Unless the resolution is a clear-cut case of you show me yours and I'll show you mine, the most likely answer is: very rarely.

Compare two managers you know; one who you believe shows

signs of strong leadership and one who shows signs of weak leadership. What are the defining traits of the stronger leader? Is it higher intelligence or an ability to assess the situation, determine the motivations of each of the protagonists and deliver a solution that has empathy with all concerned?

If your response favours higher intelligence, then you should stop right now and consider your options. In fact I would strongly urge you stop reading and expose yourself as a doyen of Mensa, because you obviously know little, or care little, about the power of EI!

Before you do, step back and consider what you've just read. Consider my last comments carefully and ask yourself another question: does what I've just written demonstrate strong EI? Or did I just assume a position of arrogance that is a little off-putting?

If you're still not sure where we're coming from, let's begin by defining what this thing called emotional intelligence is all about, and how it differs to your IQ, or Intelligence Quotient.

Simply put, your IQ is a measure of your intellectual function or capacity, or how clever you are. EQ (Emotional intelligence Quotient) measures your emotions or feelings. Where IQ is about how smart we are; EI is about how aware we are.

Emotional intelligence maps our ability to evaluate our own feelings and to be able to understand and deal with them. At the same time, emotional intelligence identifies our capacity to recognise and respond to emotions in other people. IQ uses verbal comprehension and problem solving to calculate a score, and is well suited to people with strong maths and reading skills. Emotional intelligence measures how well you understand yourself, how well you understand and deal with the emotional state in others, and how well you assess emotions in the context of the circumstances in which you are operating.

Forward thinking HR managers argue that they can assess leadership capacity in a person from their EI results. They can also assess how well they will work in a team or whether they would be a negative influence on that team. Such has been the acceptance of EI by psychologists and human resource professionals that you may find it impossible to get a job in the future without passing an EI test. In much the same way we all endured sitting our IQ tests at school to find out how much smarter, or how much dumber, we were than our classmates, employers are now using EI to discover how we might fit within an organisation's culture, or how much leadership capacity we possess.

What makes the entire debate about emotional intelligence even more compelling is that testing EI, unlike testing IQ, uses measures that rely heavily on subjective rather than objective analysis. Given its subjective nature, the war is still being waged over how you measure EI, with many still doubting how reliable the measure actually is. What doesn't appear to be in question in any quarter is that strong leaders, almost without exception, display high levels of EI.

Given this debate, Phillip Di Bella's point about my teacher is well made. IQ may measure whether you are smarter than the next person, but being smarter does not necessarily equip you for leadership, nor does it enable you to become a successful entrepreneur. IQ may give you the ability to rank yourself against others, and get you onto a rich game show, but it will not empower you to be more aware of the people around you.

***

During one of the discussions Phillip Di Bella and I had on the subject of EI, Phillip pointed to the black acrylic noticeboard on his wall where he has spelt out what EI means to him, and which he uses to mentor his directors and managers.

"For me, EI revolves around four words. The first word is **consciousness:** the ability to be conscious at all times of your surroundings, particularly what's going on and what people are doing. Next is **motivation:** the ability to understand what your motivations are, and what other people's motivations are. Third is **empathy**: to be empathetic with what's going on and not take the aggressive stance, and, finally, **context:** the ability to put everything into context."

This is a critical point in understanding for any budding intelligent entrepreneur. As we have evolved the formula for intelligent entrepreneurship throughout this book, much of what has been discussed cannot be captured as some form of empirical evidence or data. Passion is not about numbers. The Bureau of Statistics didn't help Bill Gates or Henry Ford articulate their vision. Nor can you understand what people think, or get inside their heads in order to build a powerful brand through quantitative data. The basis of this book is what some would refer to as soft data, and would reject it out of hand. But that would be to deny the intuition of people like Branson and Roddick.

This is where the going gets tough and the tough get going. Skim over this bit and you will be missing some of the most crucial links to becoming an intelligent entrepreneur.

One of the leaders in developing the concept of emotional intelligence, who many see as the world's foremost authority, is Daniel Goleman, a psychologist and prolific author. In one of his articles for the *Harvard Business Review,* he tells the story of a seasoned engineer working for a software company. The engineer and his team had been working on a project for several months and were finally presenting their proposal to the vice-president for product development. At the conclusion of the presentation, the vice-president sarcastically asked, "How long have you been out of grad school? These specifications are ridiculous."

Not long after this pronouncement, the vice-president was called away and the meeting broke up; the engineer and his team left, embarrassed and deflated, but also bitter and angry.

The engineer, obsessed about the vice-presidents remarks,

seriously considered resigning. Finally, he approached the vice-president and reminded him of the meeting, before saying, "I'm a little confused by what you were trying to accomplish. I assume you were not just trying to embarrass me – did you have some other goal in mind?"

The vice-president was stunned – he had no idea that his sarcasm, intended as a throwaway line, had been so devastating. Immediately, he apologised, conceding that he believed the plan was promising but needed work.

I discussed this story with Phillip Di Bella to see if there would be a different response from an entrepreneur to the one given by Daniel Goleman in his book. The answer is no. This is how Phillip Di Bella assessed the performance of the vice-president using his simple four-word formula of **consciousness – motivation – empathy – context.**

"Was he *conscious* of his surroundings and the work that people had been doing? I doubt it; the level of work required to bring the proposal to the stage it was at not only deserved recognition, but demanded recognition.

Was he thinking about his *motivation* or the motivation of the other people in the room when he made his remarks? Unlikely, given his response suggested a very shallow awareness of the potential power of his comment.

Did he display any level of *empathy*, not just for the people, but for their commitment to the project? He certainly didn't appear to, and his sarcasm was probably perceived to be more aggressive because of his failure to empathise.

And, finally, did he deal with the *context* of the situation? Categorically, and emphatically no, he did not. People need feedback to maintain their commitment. Feedback is the lifeblood of every organisation and needs to be clear, unequivocal and constructive."

Consider what you were doing today, before you found enough quiet time to sit down and open this book. Focus on one particular event that occurred, preferably a moment in the day when you had to make a decision; it may have been either a positive decision or a negative one. At the time, were you thinking about what your surroundings were? What was going on around you?

Stretch your mind back to where you were. What was happening in the immediate vicinity? Can you remember? Were there things happening which could have had an influence on how you made your decision? Were you aware of any particular tension in the air, or a sense of fun emanating from the people around you? Was it a positive vibe or a negative one? Perhaps you were aware of people around you working with less than their usual endeavour – or maybe harder than usual. In a word, were you *conscious* of your surroundings?

As you were in the process of making the decision, were you thinking that you had been putting it off for a while? Or maybe you had just decided to bite the bullet and act. If people were working harder than usual, did you wonder why? Or, if they were looking incredibly relaxed, did you wonder what the reason behind it was? In coming to your decision, had you inspected your grounds for making it, or whether anyone else had influenced you? Or were you acting on the spur of the moment?

Perhaps you were feeling particularly inspired or particular flat. Did any of these factors colour the way you felt towards someone or something? Were you aware of it? Did you try to change the way you approached the decision because someone provoked you? Or did you change it because someone didn't? And, finally, were you alert to not only what was going on around you but aware of all the factors which, at that very moment, could be influencing your decision? In other words, did you understand your motivation or the motivation of the people trying to influence you?

Someone with strong EI would have been able to confidently answer each of these questions in a way that identified their emotional connection with the decision. They would be careful not to isolate one part of the formula and pretend that they have tested themselves against EI and succeeded. Nor would they confuse empathy, the next part of the equation, with sympathy. Of course the two go hand in hand; empathy is an emotion centred on sympathy for someone's position or plight. You may consider a particular decision to be singularly lacking in sympathy and that a leader is not displaying empathy towards a person they are just about to sack. Think again. They may well be demonstrating a high level of empathy to the rest of the employees who may have suffered from an individual's laziness or rudeness.

***

Emotional intelligence is a complex concept that we need to keep simple. We have already alluded to the debate being waged between different groups of psychologists and researchers. There are several great books on the subject, and we urge you to read them to gain a better understanding of your own EI. Phillip Di Bella's observation at the beginning of this chapter that strong leaders are people with a strong sense of EI is equally true of intelligent entrepreneurs. What is also indisputable is that people with strong EI have the capacity to inspire and influence others, as we will discover in the next chapter.

# 17

# Emotional Leadership

If you were asked to nominate your five greatest leaders of modern times, who would you name? There may be high profile politicians, well-known business leaders, strong military leaders, even sporting leaders in your list. No matter who they are and how much your opinion differs from a friend's list, or your partner's, the one thing each of the leaders you nominate will have in common is your respect and admiration. If they don't, why are they on your list?

Your list might contain household names like Martin Luther King and Muhammad Ali, who both featured prominently in the early stages of this book. Maybe you would include a number of politicians, such as Bob Hawke, John Howard, Margaret Thatcher or John F Kennedy. Or perhaps you may be more inclined to nominate Angela Merkel or Ronald Reagan, even Mahatma Gandhi or Israel's "iron lady", the feisty Golda Meir. Maybe Sir Winston Churchill gets a guernsey as both a politician and a military leader; perhaps Weary Dunlop or General George Patton, or Field Marshall Rommel, maybe even Julius Caesar would be among the military leaders you respect. Pope John Paul II is consistently rated as one of the world's great modern leaders, and not wanting to suggest any kind of link, except they are in the same sentence, Mao Zedong and Hitler each earned enormous respect from their followers, but massive vilification from the rest of the world.

I would be particularly interested to see who you include on your list as business leaders; perhaps Bill Gates or Steve Jobs, maybe Oprah Winfrey, Richard Branson and Anita Roddick, or, closer to home, Janine Allis or Dick Smith. I would also be intrigued to know how many of them you would define as both a leader and as an entrepreneur.

At a recent strategic planning meeting, Phillip Di Bella spent some time discussing with his senior management the distinction between leaders and managers. He asked his team to articulate what they saw as the difference. There was complete agreement in the room that management is largely about process, while leadership, it was argued, is defined more by attitude and behaviour. Good managers apply planning tools learnt on the job or through some form of skills training. Good managers apply tested procedures and processes, and verify outcomes against known criteria. It was also agreed amongst the group that good leaders demonstrate strong management skills, but that managers were not necessarily great leaders.

In the end, it was agreed that leadership skills are less tangible.

Authors like Stephen Covey argue that leadership is about trust, while other authors focus on other human traits, such as inspiration, manifested through our character and emotional capabilities.

In the Di Bella Coffee directors' meeting, there was unanimous agreement that management skills could be acquired, but there was not quite the same confidence about being able to acquire leadership skills.

This debate about nurture or nature is not new. Nor is the genuine dilemma about whether people can learn to become an intelligent entrepreneur.

The story about John Macarthur, mentioned earlier, was a deliberate diversion. The history books describe Macarthur as a wool pioneer. I think a more accurate description would be wool entrepreneur, but even that would have been to sell him short.

Macarthur came to NSW as an officer in the New South Wales

Corps, with the responsibility to protect and police the new colony. From all reports, he was a strong leader, yet there is nothing in his upbringing that would suggest leadership was his destiny. He was not born into a life of privilege; was the son of a humble draper. At 15 he was commissioned as an ensign in Fish's Corps, a regiment of the British Army formed to fight in the American War of Independence. Either by good luck or good management the war was over before the regiment sailed and, still a teenager, Macarthur retired on half pay, to a farm in Devon, where he took advantage of his good fortune and began self-educating.

That was his lot for the next five years. Who knows what he read or learned during that time, but there are various reports that he was considering either a life as a farmer or a life at the bar. Instead, he returned to the army, and a posting to NSW.

On his arrival in the new colony, he was summoned to the governor's office to be offered the position of Commandant of Parramatta. Three years later, Macarthur was granted 100 acres by the acting Governor, Major Francis Grose. A year later, he received a further grant of 100 acres for being the first man to clear and cultivate 50 acres of land. He named the property Elizabeth Farm, in honour of his wife.

Macarthur began his wool dynasty experimenting in improving wool quality by successfully cross-breeding hair-bearing Bengal ewes from India with Irish wool rams. Emboldened by his early success, he called on two friends, commanders of supply ships sent to the Cape for provisions, to purchase any quality sheep they could find and bring them back to NSW.

The two ship's captains managed to procure a number of prized pure Merino sheep, originally from the King of Spain's jealously guarded flock, but at the time impounded as part of a dispute in a southern African colony. The pure Merino wool that Macarthur managed to produce from the new additions to his own flock was considered equal to anything produced out of Spain.

Other opportunities fell the way of Macarthur, but it would be foolish to think his fortune was simply luck or being in the right place at the right time. He actively cultivated more than just his sheep. He sought favour from well-placed sponsors and patrons, including the British Colonial Secretary, Lord Camden. By 1801 Macarthur was the largest sheep breeder in the colony, judiciously helped along by a grant from Lord Camden of 5,000 acres of prime grazing land on the banks of the Nepean River.

Macarthur was also the wealthiest man in the colony. He became a highly successful horse breeder and established the first commercial vineyard. In 1825 he entered the NSW Legislative Council and served until 1832, when he was forced to retire due to ill health. Australia's most prominent entrepreneur of the 18th and 19th centuries, whose face adorned the first two dollar note in the new Australian decimal currency, passed away in 1834, leaving a legacy for his new country which may never be surpassed.

Had Macarthur discovered the formula for entrepreneurial intelligence? When he took early retirement to self-educate, was that a stroke of luck or an opportunity? At 16 or 17, did Macarthur set about creating a vision to be the wealthiest man in NSW? Sitting at his desk in the small farmhouse in Devon, did he envision a future place where wool would become the perfect industry for a new colony? A commodity that could tolerate the extremes of being shipped half way round the world; that would be able to take advantage of the Napoleonic Wars, cutting off supply of wool from Spain to his beloved England?

Of course he didn't. To suggest so is absurd in the extreme. Macarthur's vision evolved as the man evolved. His passion was obvious, as was his disdain for fools, or for authority that failed to look beyond its own narrow-minded interests. Short of inventing the word, he also understood the power of his brand. Merino wool is still considered to be one of the finest natural fibres ever created.

You tell me, was Macarthur's entrepreneurial success and his role as a leader nurture or nature?

Now, look at your list of who you consider to be the five greatest leaders of modern times and ask yourself how many of them were born leaders. Or perhaps the question should be: how many of them do you believe saw themselves as natural leaders at an early age? If you could ask each one of the people on your list either of those questions, do you think their answer would be a confident "you bet!" or a more considered, "not sure."

Regardless of who is on your list, they are most likely there because they have moved you in some way. We're not in a position to define why, but we are very confident that the leaders you have chosen have had the ability to spur your passion, to inspire you. It's unlikely you will know much about Martin Luther King, except what you read in the history books or what you have seen in documentaries about the struggle against racism. I was too young to be close to his passion, but it was impossible not to be moved by the man's emotional engagement with his cause.

John F Kennedy was a politician whose passion and oratory skills lifted him above the ruck long before an assassin's bullets ensured his place in history. Bill Clinton and Barack Obama are other American Presidents who have the oratory skills to motivate, as had Paul Keating in Australia. But do they all share a similar level of passion, whatever their cause, as Martin Luther King?

What separates the leaders on your list from the rest of the population? Were they born with those attributes or did they acquire them through upbringing? Or is it a combination of both? Without question, each one is nominated because of their ability to influence and motivate others through the spoken word. Obama is a particularly gifted orator, as is Paul Keating. But is a flair for speaking in public a defining sign of leadership? You might struggle with the idea of getting up in front of a roomful of people, but I promise you, good public speakers are as much a product of learned behaviour as they are born to it.

Vision and passion are both accorded high marks in all the articles on leadership. Martin Luther King had a vision that inspired a nation to monumental change. Gates and Jobs both were able to articulate a vision powerful enough to drive their respective organisations to the very top of the international list of great corporations. Then again, as we remarked in a different part of this story, Hitler had a clear vision of what he wanted Germany to be, and he had the passion and oratory skills to sell it to the populace.

Phillip Di Bella has no doubts that a person's capacity to create a powerful vision is in large part a matter of confidence, and huge part passion, and just a little bit of emotional intelligence.

"No one taps you on the shoulder and anoints you as a leader. Leadership is something you earn, and I have no doubt that a person's ability to be a strong leader is enhanced ten-fold when they become more conscious of their EI capacity."

What stands out in the work on emotional intelligence, by people such as Daniel Goleman, is that not only can leadership traits be identified, but the level of emotional intelligence in a person increases the higher that person is on the leadership scale.

So, can you learn how to become a better leader? The answer, of course, is "yes!"

When was the last time you laughed at a mistake you had made, or used self-deprecating humour to lighten the mood of a meeting or a conversation? If you answer "frequently", then there is a very good chance that you have a high level of self-awareness, and, as a consequence, have taken a very positive step towards being a strong leader. If your answer is "no", all is not lost – you just might have to work a little harder.

# 18

# The missing link

While researching this book, I came across a paper written by a couple of Australian academics, just one small paper amongst a pile of articles, books, dissertations, theses and printed downloads from numerous Google searches. There is so much information out there about entrepreneurs and what makes them successful it is frightening. If you don't believe me simply Google terms like 'entrepreneurial leadership' and see how many hits you come up with. Then, if you have the time, inclination or interest, start reading, I can promise you it will be several hours later before you lift your gaze from the computer screen.

The paper was titled *The untold story: is the entrepreneur of the 21st century defined by emotional intelligence?*[7] and was a refreshing breath of fresh air amongst the rest. Written in 2003 by two academics, Bernadette Cross and Anthony Travaglione, from Newcastle University, the research endeavoured to define what sets entrepreneurs apart from other business owners.

I had become used to reading academic papers that approached the subject using dry, structured narrative, where words of less than four syllables were the exception, not the rule. I was also used to reading papers where the researchers would frame their findings in language that was so cautious that it would offend the most pedantic lawyer.

Bottom line: I was almost tempted not to read the paper, but I'm very glad I did.

Even more fortuitous was the timing of my discovery. I had just received a highly confidential report from Phillip Di Bella, which had been commissioned by his HR department. Phillip had wanted each of his senior directors to take part in a program that could provide a comprehensive interpretation of a person's leadership potential based on their emotional intelligence. Phillip's own report made not only fascinating reading, but it brought the findings of the Newcastle academics into sharp focus.

The methodology used by Cross and Travaglione was qualitative, using structured, in-depth interviews with a small number of high profile Australian entrepreneurs.

The five participants were Dr Peter Farrell, Cindy Luken, Professor Carl Wood, Richard Owens, and Paul Cave. You may or may not know their names immediately, but we can assure you they are an impressive line-up of eminent Australians.

Dr Peter Farrell is the founder of ResMed, a global manufacturer of products for the treatment of sleep disorders, particularly obstructive sleep apnoea.

ResMed employs about 2700 employees worldwide and has direct operations in 18 countries and distribution in more than 50 countries. The company is currently reported to be turning over more than USD$ 1 billion. Peter Farrell was the 2000 National Winner of the Australian Entrepreneur of the Year.

Cindy Luken is the founder and chair of the gourmet biscuit company Luken & May, which she started in her kitchen in the late 90s. Within a small number of years the company was turning over AUD$6 million p.a. and Cindy was inducted into the Australian Businesswomen's Hall of Fame.

Professor Carl Wood was a prominent Australian gynaecologist, best known for his pioneering work developing and commercialising the technique of in vitro fertilisation. He was instrumental in the world's first IVF pregnancy, the first IVF birth from the use of donor eggs, the first birth from frozen embryo donor, and Australia's first IVF surrogate birth. Professor Wood passed away in 2011 having achieved international recognition for his work both as a medical researcher and as a brilliant entrepreneur.

Richard Owens developed a chain of 45 Food Barn supermarkets across Australia, which was to later become the Bi-Lo operation. At their peak, the chain was turning over $220 million. Richard Owens is now part of the wine growing industry, in one of Australia's premium wine growing regions, the Hunter Valley.

Last but not least, Paul Cave is the founder and chairman of BridgeClimb, the company that provides climb experiences to the top of the Sydney Harbour Bridge. Close on 3 million visitors from over 137 countries have climbed the SHB since Cave won a hard fought battle with the authorities to allow the licence to proceed. Since then, he has won the plaudits of the tourism industry and won such awards as the best major tourist attraction at the Australian Tourism Awards, and recognition from Lonely Planet as one of the world's top 10 Biggest Adrenaline Rush experiences.

As the title of their paper suggests, the authors wanted to answer the question: is the new form of intelligence, emotional intelligence (EI, or EQ), the untold story behind entrepreneurship? To put some context around their answer, they commenced their paper with a review of the genesis of emotional intelligence, identifying the different contributors and theories across the last twenty to thirty years. They acknowledged the work done by psychologists and scientists who had begun this journey by investigating the science of social intelligence, defined as the ability to understand and manage people. The authors also engaged in a level of scientific debate about the credentials of the various luminaries in the field, including Mayer, Caruso and Salovey, and Goleman.

Frankly, none of that discussion excited me; I'd already read much of the work. It was only when the authors started to examine the responses of the five entrepreneurs to their original hypothesis using an integrated questionnaire based on the original Mayer, Caruso and Salovey EQ model and the more populist Goleman EQ Workplace model that I reached for Phillip Di Bella's confidential EI report.

In a nutshell, what the researchers found was that each of the entrepreneurs they interviewed showed a significantly high level of overall emotional intelligence, as well as strong results in all of the sub-sections of emotional intelligence.

The researchers were quick to stress that their study did not prove that EI was a critical criteria essential to strong entrepreneurship, and it would be wrong of us to suggest otherwise. While we're in the mood for confessions we also have to stress that the theory behind entrepreneurial intelligence is equally unproven; ultimately you have to make your own mind up about whether the lessons to be had are worth the paper they are written on.

The EI report completed by Phillip Di Bella is a confidential and trademarked document so it is not appropriate for me to divulge the detail here. Suffice to say that although the language and procedures used in any EI test vary, their intention and purpose are fundamentally the same. This particular report uses a range of emotional competencies as a set of measurable characteristics related to the individual's effective performance in a specific circumstance. In this particular reporting procedure, the authors use various scientific studies that link emotional intelligence to effective leadership.

The candidate is required to provide answers to a range of questions, which are then scored against ratings that indicate the level of effort required to reach an acceptable score, or rate whether the subject has exceeded what is determined as an effective range. The scores are then shown on a scale of rankings that show significant strengths at one end and obvious weaknesses at the other. In each instance the authors align the results to known emotional intelligence criteria.

Since Daniel Goleman first introduced his concept of emotional intelligence, most of the elements of every model or testing procedure used have fit within the four generic domains of self-awareness, self-management, social awareness and relationship management. Each model endeavours to establish a point of difference, either through language or extension, but the final assessment still comes back to the four core elements.

In the confidential report that Phillip Di Bella showed me, the first competency defined emotionally intelligent leaders as being aware of their emotional experience and aware of what they were feeling most of the time, which, in turn gave them the capacity to recognise how their feelings and emotions impacted on their personal opinions.

Nine further competencies expand on the four core elements of EI: identifying the importance of self-confidence, self-reliance, self-actualisation, openness, relationship building, empathy, self-control and adaptability.

In total, the report assesses each person's EI across ten competencies. Phillip Di Bella's results are exceptional. In six of the categories, Phillip scored at the top of the ratings scale, in two other categories he scored at the top end of the second range, while his score in the remaining two competencies was still higher than the median score. Of course, for anyone reading this book the real question is does Phillip's EI report support or contradict the findings of the Newcastle University academics?

*** 

In an analysis of the results, the authors of the research paper – *The Untold Story* – confirm that the five entrepreneurs they interviewed displayed all the hallmarks of strong emotional intelligence, that is, they all showed significant emotional self-awareness and high levels of awareness of the emotions in others. Importantly, the authors were able to put to one side the debate surrounding modelling, by showing that regardless of which model was used, Goleman, or Mayer, Caruso and Salovey, the entrepreneurs in the study, achieved high EI scores in both. Not only are the results impressive, they correlate closely with our belief that intelligent entrepreneurs have very high levels of emotional intelligence.

This is what the authors wrote in their summary:

"Each (entrepreneur) showed significant emotional self-awareness and awareness of the emotions in others. For example they were particularly adept at understanding their strengths and weaknesses involving emotion. It was evident that all the entrepreneurs had to have high level of understanding of others, not only of verbal expression, but also non-verbal expression of emotion."

Based on the competency scales of the EI report undertaken by Phillip Di Bella, it is impossible not to conclude that the five entrepreneurs in the study would have scored in similar ranges to Phillip. Not only did the five reveal significant levels of emotional self-awareness and awareness of the emotions in others, they showed higher than average EI through:

- High levels of understanding and insight into others, through both verbal and non-verbal expressions of emotion, such as withdrawal and silence;
- The capacity to set up a work environment where 'the cards are on the table' and where expressions of emotion are part of the workplace strategy;
- Proactive engagement with employees about their emotions, including the use of emotion to resolve issues;
- Prioritising self-control, particularly in a workplace where ambiguity, obstacles, emotional chaos and workplace stress are commonplace;
- The use of emotional reactions to criticisms and rejection to find better solutions;

- Regarding setbacks as a challenge, in fact accepting setbacks as normal, transforming them into a positive reason for improvement;
- Turning anxiety into determination and relentlessness, while using frustration as a motivator;
- Understanding and treating each person as an individual who needs individual attention;
- Exhibiting an exceptional amount of well-grounded self-confidence, and a realistic assessment of their own abilities;
- The determination to delay gratification, while still able to quickly recover from stress;
- The use of emotions to motivate, and,
- Cultivating rapport among employees and clients.

When Phillip Di Bella simplified the idea of EI down to four words – consciousness, motivation, empathy and context – he was effectively summarising all the key points highlighted by the research. His results from the EI report not only confirm that he understands the importance of EI, but they also reinforce the high level of emotional intelligence he brings to his business. While his scores point to strong self-sufficiency and autonomy, they reinforce his preparedness as an individual to take charge. While scoring strongly in his ability to both present and protect his own views, he scored equally well in demonstrating his respect for others, even if that required challenging the views of others. And while Phillip's communication and relationship skills were seen as one of his signature strengths, he also demonstrated high regard for other people's feelings.

All that remains is to answer the simple question: do you have a high level of emotional intelligence? If not, can you learn, or can someone teach you, how to become more emotionally intelligent? The answer is an unequivocal yes. But only you can come up with the motivation to start learning.

# 19

## The ultimate coffee experience

When Phillip Di Bella founded Di Bella Coffee in 2002, his ambition was to help his customers achieve the perfect cup of coffee every time. His vision was a place where the experience of enjoying coffee would be applauded as the ultimate experience – the ultimate coffee experience.

A bold vision, you say, but is it really that bold?

In listing alternatives for 'ultimate' the *Collins Thesaurus* leaves us in no doubt about its meaning: supreme, highest, greatest, maximum, paramount, most significant, superlative.

That's a tough ask in anyone's language.

Consider the most obvious implications of such a vision. If you were to sit down today to plan the steps to get to a future place, what do you think would be the most critical market issues, or the most pressing financial factors, that would influence your decisions or planning?

Henry Ford wanted to democratise the automobile. Implicit in his vision was the need to find ways to make motor cars affordable to the average American. He didn't doubt that there was a market need. Everything he did was focused on cost efficiencies; smarter production methods; lighter, cheaper, metals for fabrication; simpler operating systems. The list goes on, but the decisions were straightforward once he'd aligned them to his vision.

Bill Gates could see a place where there was a computer on every desk and in every home. In other words, fewer geeks and more mums and dads and schoolchildren using computers every day, maybe not 24/7, but then again, maybe one day, who knows? The answer to Gates' vision is almost as transparent as Fords' – an affordable operating system that everyone can use, anywhere, anytime.

The results speak for themselves. At the height of the introduction of Office 2010, Microsoft estimated that one person was buying a copy somewhere in the world every second. The same product pushed the number of users of Microsoft operating systems to over a billion worldwide. Estimates vary, but many observers claim that Microsoft has a 90% share of the software market around the globe.

Once you've set the vision clearly, the strategic decisions should be self-evident. If they're not, you need to re-think the vision. When Phillip Di Bella accepted the invitation to sell coffee at Jan Powers Farmers' Markets in New Farm he had already determined that his future business was in roasting and wholesale. That was a strategic decision that flowed from his vision of the ultimate coffee experience. Without question that's where he saw the greatest opportunities, but to understand why, we need to understand Phillip's early career and the circumstances that helped shape both his vision and his pathway to achieve it.

*** 

Brisbane's Fortitude Valley is a vastly different place now than it was in the 1980s and 90s. Today it is a thriving, cosmopolitan part of Brisbane, home of one of the best music scenes in the country, with bragging rights to bands like Powderfinger, who cut their teeth in the frenetic cauldron between Ann and Wickham Streets. In recent years, the Valley has undergone a facelift. A government-led urban renewal campaign has encouraged high density residential development, and the people who live there can now be seen out and about enjoying the benefits of inner city living.

In the 80s and 90s it was a different beast entirely. The rise of suburban shopping centres largely put an end to what had been one of Australia's busiest shopping precincts. David Jones, Myer and the now defunct Waltons had all been prominent. David Jones was the first to close its doors, with Myer following in the early 1980s. What had been a thriving commercial centre became a neglected, in some places dilapidated, shell of its previous bustling life. To add to the insult, the 1980s was the decade of the Fitzgerald Inquiry into graft and corruption in the Queensland police force. Much of the focus of the Inquiry was on the Valley, which had achieved notoriety as Brisbane's red light district and as the home to many of the city's illegal gambling houses.

In 1992, at the age of 17, Phillip Di Bella was hired as a chef at the Cosmopolitan Café, in Brunswick Street, in the very heart of the Valley. The Cosmo, as it was known by the locals, had begun its life in 1975, quickly earning a reputation for cheap breakfasts, pizzas and good coffee. Adding to its appeal, the Cosmo usually stayed open until 4am and had been a favourite meeting spot for many of the characters who enriched the seedier aspects of the Valley's reputation.

Today, we take for granted what a good cup of coffee should taste like. We've outgrown the chemical taste of most instant coffee and are generally at ease in ordering a latte or a piccolo or an espresso, and even know what we mean when we order a double shot. But it wasn't always the case. Even in the early 90s, when Phillip took up his employ at the Cosmo many would still order a cappuccino without having any real appreciation of the skills of a good barista, and still insist on pouring in the sugar. But we were learning.

It's not hard to imagine the scene at the Cosmo. The old school Italian immigrants would sit in a corner of the shop talking among themselves, shaking their heads at the antics and requests of some of the 'amateur' coffee drinkers – if you didn't drink it black, you didn't rate. But still the queue for cappuccinos and piccolos and lattes would grow longer each day,

Phillip Di Bella became immersed in the business of making good coffee. His clientele included coffee lovers from across Brisbane. They came in all shapes and sizes; they included the rich, and the homeless off the streets. Phillip became an adept barista, and then graduated to being one of the best in Brisbane. Those who watched him work his magic at the espresso machine, and then tasted the results, were besotted. First timers, cajoled and berated by their friends into coming, were instant devotees once they tasted the coffee Phillip conjured up. In twenty plus years, Phillip estimates he has drawn over a million cups of coffee from an espresso machine, and that number still gets bigger every day.

He learnt everything he could about coffee beans; where they came from and the different flavours each region produced. He had a keen sense of smell and taste and could detect the difference between beans from Ethiopia and those from New Guinea, the difference between beans from Puerto Rica and those from Mexico. When he began roasting beans, he experimented, and discovered how to get the best flavours through medium or dark roasting. He learnt to trust his senses, particular his sense of smell and his palate, and knew exactly, by the smell of sugar caramelising or the whiff of a bean about to burn, when to end a roast.

Phillip also watched what was happening around him, and learnt about people. He observed how the other baristas dealt with the customers, the way some made the customers feel comfortable while others were more abrupt. He decided what he liked and what he didn't like about customer service. And what he liked was the style of service he would want himself. He started to recognise that the customers responded when he shared knowledge with them, when he engaged with them above and beyond the level of making them a great cup of coffee. So he increased his energy level to make sure he interacted. The regulars responded to his efforts and kept coming back, and back, and back …

After a few years at Cosmo, Phillip was an accomplished barista and roaster. He had developed very good and insightful people skills. He was already training new staff to a high level of competence and was managing customer complaints like a veteran. The reputation of Cosmo was steadily climbing throughout Brisbane, thanks in no small part to Phillip's touch.

At its peak, Cosmo was selling 1000 kilograms of roasted coffee beans per week, not only to satisfy the growing demand of their regulars but to supply many of the cafes around Brisbane. Phillip supervised the roasting; making sure nothing was ever burnt or wasted. He developed networks amongst the owners of other cafes they sold coffee to. He even helped many of them to develop their own businesses, with tips and ideas he had successfully implemented at the Cosmo. His knowledge of roasting and of business was growing daily, and so was the owner's reliance on Phillip. Finally, he was invited to take over the core business, and in response Phillip lifted his energy to another level entirely.

Unfortunately, there is an unpleasant side to the nine years Phillip spent at the Cosmo. Frankly, I don't believe the story is necessarily part of this book except in the way that the circumstances may have shaped Phillip's approach to his business and his vision.

Gianna Di Bella is Phillip's wife. She is one of the most gracious people you will ever meet, a wonderful mother, highly intelligent, with a Masters in Psychology, and beautiful. She is also the estranged daughter of Benito Di Felice, the then owner of the Cosmopolitan.

Gianna had worked closely with her father, even helping him restructure his loans to free up cash to build the business. While Gianna and employees like Phillip worked hard to make the Cosmo a success, Benito Di Felice had become perhaps a little too reliant on others, and in the process allowed his attention to wander. With time on his hands, he fell in love with one of his employees.

His new love was not popular with the other staff. She used her relationship with the owner to establish her own position, and managed to drive a wedge between father and daughter. Her treatment of staff became so poisoned that formal complaints were lodged by staff members with the Industrial Relations Commission. In the aftermath of Gianna's efforts to restructure her father's loans, Di Felice's new love accused her of stealing money from him.

Phillip and Gianna did not become romantically linked until many years after he had started working for Cosmo. Their attraction for each other meant they spent many hours together, inevitably talking about what was happening at work. Things were rapidly coming to a head. Phillip was contacted by Industrial Relations as a consequence of the complaints other employees had made about the way they were treated. He was asked to give evidence in court to support the allegations.

A short time later Phillip received a message from Di Felice saying he was fired. Phillip subsequently learned that Di Felice had accused him of sabotaging the coffee bean roaster, and intended to sue. Phillip categorically denied the claim. Later again, it emerged that Di Felice had been attempting to roast beans when he accidentally set fire to the roaster. And so the die was cast.

There is no question in my mind that a key part of Phillip's strength is his capacity to observe, to listen, to learn. He spent nearly a decade working at the Cosmopolitan, watching and listening to everything that was going on around him. He learnt about the good, and he watched and learnt from the bad. Regrettably, but, perhaps, fortuitously, the experience at the Cosmo was often bitter and filled with acrimony, but it was always a learning curve and it provided Phillip with a wide palette of experiences.

He was relied upon heavily by Di Felice. The owner rarely touched the roaster, and any skills he had in that direction were left to wither. He allowed Phillip to develop their customer base and their customers' loyalty. He encouraged Phillip to undertake the buying of green beans and to develop the blends they served their customers. To Phillip's credit, while there is no doubt that the Cosmo was a tough school, he still insists that had his father-in-law not turned on him he would most likely still be there, and that today Cosmo would be one of the biggest coffee businesses in the country. Instead, Phillip and Gianna established Di Bella Coffee.

It was during the years Phillip spent at Cosmo that he began to shape his vision of that elusive future place. He had seen first-hand the delight people took in the simple pleasure that was coffee. He knew from experience that his customers were not only the wealthy, or the elite, but that they also included police officers and prostitutes, office workers and professional people, and some of his customers lived on the street and hoarded their pennies to buy a great coffee experience.

He built customer loyalty for a product that cost less than $2 a cup in the 90s.

To create his vision, Phillip used the same skills he employed to learn his craft:

"Defining your own vision begins with looking and listening. You look and listen to the situation around you, and then you look and listen to what's inside you. You must look and listen with your senses to be impartial; look and listen with your mind to be practical; look and listen with your heart to know your feelings; and you must look and listen with your soul to allow the whole vision to incubate and grow."

If you relate Phillip's advice to his vision of the ultimate coffee experience you begin to see not only the sense of it, but the strategies that would make it happen. Phillip Di Bella's vision was 100% customer focused in the same way all great visions are focused. Vision is not about "me" it is about satisfying a customer need better than anyone else has been able to. Ford's vision was completely focused on his customers. Everything he did was to deliver a customer experience that could be enjoyed and appreciated. Every step he took to reduce the heavy manufacturing costs and heavy dependence on craftsmen was not to diminish the experience of his customers but to enable them to engage with the experience, because his only viable outcome was to produce a motor vehicle without any option for inferior workmanship. And core to achieving his vision was automation, before the word was even invented.

Phillip Di Bella's vision to create the ultimate coffee experience was a vision created entirely for people who appreciated great coffee. He never doubted that he had a market, that a need existed. He had spent nine years of his life understanding the appreciation people had for a very good cup of coffee. In his mind was a very clear picture of what would be required to reach this future place. It was also a vision with a large dollop of passion.

Phillip explains it this way:

> "I have always been driven by passion and knowledge. Knowledge and education are power, and passion is the most powerful driver of all. The key to making great coffee is to understand the capabilities and qualities of your products and equipment, and to apply that knowledge to achieve the result you want: the ultimate coffee experience."

To achieve his vision, Phillip developed a business strategy that set out what would be required to control each step of the pathway to delivering the ultimate coffee experience. He even gave his strategy a name; he called it "My Crop to Cup".

# 20

# MC₂C – the magic formula

The first time I watched Phillip Di Bella make a cup of coffee was in his boardroom. We had only recently met and I was there to discuss with him the Di Bella Coffee brand. An impressive commercial coffee machine dominates one end of the boardroom. It's not just there for show; it is kept in pristine condition for just such a meeting and is regularly used to sample new blends. When Phillip finished making my coffee, he handed me the cup with the words, "Every cup of coffee has a story."

As I have come to expect from Phillip, he spoke with a great deal of passion about a subject he knows a great deal about.

"The story of that cup actually starts in one of the remotest parts of the Amazon jungle. That's where some of the green beans used in the blend you're drinking come from. We buy a substantial amount of coffee from Brazil, which is famous for producing a polished, full bodied and good looking coffee with medium to high acidity."

Phillip talked to me with the consummate practice of someone used to talking to people who probably know very little, if anything, about coffee. At the time, I knew what I liked, and not much else. I'd never even thought about the origins of coffee before this meeting. So, while I sat back and enjoyed my latte, Phillip continued to weave the magic of his story.

"In all, we buy green beans from ten different countries in Central and South America."

I asked why. His response was not condescending in the least, even though he'd probably been asked the same question a thousand times before.

"Almost every country is different and unique. Brazilian coffee is very similar to Costa Rican, but less aromatic. Columbian coffee has a beautiful hazelnut taste. El Salvador grows coffee at high altitude, which produces a well-balanced sweetness. By way of contrast, coffee in Guatemala is grown at low altitudes, which results in a bean that is not only sweet and delicate but intensely aromatic as well. People fond of licorice love coffee blended from beans from Honduras, and if you love chocolate, the best South American beans with a tendency towards chocolate are from Peru. Of course, if you're a real chocaholic then you would probably prefer the beans from Ethiopia."

At this point I couldn't help breaking in with the admission that I had no idea coffee was grown in Ethiopia, or that coffee connoisseurs talked a similar language to wine connoisseurs. Phillip laughed.

"Ethiopia is the birthplace of coffee. It's where it all began thousands of years ago. That country holds a special connection for anyone in the business. Today we purchase a significant amount of beans from growers in Ethiopia, as we do from 15 other countries across the world. Apart from Central and South America and Ethiopia, we buy beans from India, Indonesia, Kenya, Papua New Guinea and Tanzania. Your comparison with wine connoisseurs is a fair one. Every one of the countries I mentioned offers something different for our blends, the same way different grape varieties offer different flavours and textures for wine producers. Some of the differences are broad; others are more subtle. The African countries, almost without exception, produce coffee beans with a strong emphasis on fruity, winey flavours and a hint of spice.

"In the same way that a wine vintner looks to create something special, my priority has always been to deliver a consistently excellent cup of coffee through our own unique, or, what I would call, our signature blends, a process that starts long before we buy any beans.

"First we decide what we want the blend to achieve in terms of taste parameters and profile." Phillip acknowledged my blank expression and explained, "By profile I'm talking about the level of acidity, the body, aroma, maybe the level of sweetness that we want to achieve. Once we have that clear we then go in search of the beans we require to achieve it."

I have spent most of my life helping companies build their brands and have been privy to many great success stories. I have learnt a great deal about a diverse and wide range of different products and services. I have been fortunate enough to fly in the jump seats of commercial airliners and sit in on boardroom lunches of the biggest oil companies. I have visited exotic locations and dined with general managers of five-star hotels, and have sat alongside the driver/operator of the world's largest dragline in an open cut coal mine. I have toured confectionary, corn chip and biscuit manufacturing plants, walked through cane fields and visited sugar mills, and been tutored on the various diseases that afflict mango trees.

Trust has been an important part of my life, and, once earned, it allows you to be privy to some of the most captivating stories you could ever wish to hear. For me, every one of these stories is a privilege and a fascination. They are stories that define what makes a company unique or shows what its point of difference is. The story that was unfolding as Phillip discussed the complexities of coffee was another fascinating journey for me. It was also the start of my education about coffee, and how the Di Bella Coffee brand has achieved a unique place amongst specialty coffee companies. The story Phillip calls "My Crop to Cup", or MC2C, is compelling, and is a fascinating insight for future entrepreneurs.

***

From the very outset, Phillip Di Bella determined that to create a powerful brand he needed to be in control of as much of his supply chain as possible. Without control, he reasoned, it would be nigh on impossible to deliver on the promise of the ultimate coffee experience.

The starting place was the growers themselves.

Di Bella Coffee employs its own Green Bean specialists to work directly with growers in the sixteen different bean-growing countries across the globe. Their goal is to ensure only the highest quality crops are selected. Once Phillip and his team have decided what they want to achieve with a particular blend, they then determine which coffee beans would provide those flavours, and which farms, regardless of which country, or which part of the world they are in, grow those varieties. Those farms are then shortlisted.

With over a dozen signature blends that Di Bella Coffee supplies year round, it is no mean feat to maintain consistency. The different seasons and the varying crops across the world require careful evaluation and judgement. The specialists employed by Di Bella Coffee need to understand how the different soils and climates impact on the coffee bean and what effect will be achieved by harvesting and processing techniques. To succeed, Di Bella Coffee must stay in constant touch with farmers to be sure they will have the right beans to consistently meet their blend profiles.

Phillip Di Bella believes that the foundation of any passion is education, which, in turn, means knowledge. This becomes evident at every level of the Di Bella Coffee business. The Green Bean specialists need to understand the vagaries of what they are working with in planting, harvesting and processing. They also need to understand the pressures on market prices. Prices are set by the farmers, based on the quality of each lot. Other factors influence and shape market value – the quality of beans, the cost of production, expected return on investment, even the price of coffee on the futures market and the differential between the American and Australian Dollars.

Di Bella Coffee doesn't haggle with its partners. The company's goal is to maintain goodwill, preferring to negotiate a fair and substantial price for the farmers to encourage them to constantly strive for higher quality. But the Di Bella team still needs to know their business inside out. Once the beans have been selected, shipped and are in the warehouse, the next step in the fulfilment of the Di Bella Coffee brand promise takes place.

\*\*\*

"For any quality wholesaler, consistency is the key."

Phillip stood next to the 120 kilo Petroncini roaster he had custom made in Italy to very exacting specifications.

"We use a cast iron drum instead of stainless steel, which most other models use. That way we can get maximum stability in our heat control. Even the 2kg sample roaster we used to batch test small amounts of coffee is made and calibrated to the same specifications as the bulk roasters."

This is the kind of attention to detail that is central to this entire book. It is a demonstration of the passion Phillip brings to his craft; it is a commitment to delivering what Phillip defines as his vision – the ultimate coffee experience. And it is the power which he brings to his brand – the consistency of a promise which otherwise would be allowed to drift.

That commitment continues to grow at each phase of the operation.

"Our goal is to deliver coffee to our customers as close to roasting as possible." Phillip pointed to a delivery being prepared for a wholesale customer. "To meet our 'fresh is best' policy, all coffee for our wholesale accounts is roasted to order, ensuring they receive fresh coffee within 7 days of roasting.

"Di Bella coffee never sits on a shelf going stale. As soon as we receive a shipment from overseas it is blended with other beans, moving swiftly through production from roasting to packing, ready for despatch across the country." Phillip pointed to the adjoining retail operation through the glass viewing windows he had installed so that customers could see what was happening in the roasting warehouse. "All our coffee for our retail operations is roasted daily to ensure a constant supply of the freshest beans in all our blends."

We walked through to the packing area and once again Phillip's commitment to his vision and his brand was obvious.

"Everything is packaged immediately after roasting to ensure absolute freshness. We designed the packaging equipment to package the coffee quickly and effectively without breaking or crushing the beans."

I picked up one of the bags and remarked on the date on the bag.

Phillip's reply went to the heart of it. "We date every blend we send out so our customers can check for themselves the freshness of their product. That's part of what gives me confidence in being able to tell our customers that their customers will be getting the ultimate coffee experience."

\*\*\*

Phillip Di Bella doesn't rest on his laurels once the detail is locked down in purchase, roasting and packaging. Just as important as the finest blends, roasted with a keen nose and sense of taste for a great coffee experience, is the education necessary to ensure that the human element of making coffee is as well prepared as it can be (there's that word education again!).

In the conclusion to the "My Crop to Cup" handbook, Phillip Di Bella writes about how he is driven by passion and education.

"The driver of everything we do is passion, and the strategy with which we apply our passion is education. The key to making great coffee is knowing the capabilities and qualities of your products and equipment, and applying this knowledge to achieve the result you want: your ultimate coffee experience ...”

The Di Bella team is constantly educating. On the road, Business Development Managers don't just sell coffee; they are constantly working with wholesale customers to increase their knowledge and expertise. Baristas are shown the latest techniques, and given invaluable tips on how to improve their delivery. From their initial training, every barista who serves a Di Bella Coffee latte or cappuccino, or espresso, short black or long black is taught the skills required to deliver the ultimate coffee experience.

They are shown how to treat their work area as the ultimate production line, with everything in its correct place to ensure an uncluttered and efficient workflow. Di Bella Coffee provides wholesale customers with advice on what equipment to use, but it does not dictate. What it provides is the support to make sure whatever coffee making equipment the café or restaurant owner chooses that the products and the barista's training is of a standard to ensure the required outcome. Phillip's mantra on this echoes the old adage that you should never blame your tools.

"A good barista can work on any machine, while a bad barista can produce bad coffee on any machine. The very best coffee making equipment will never make up for lack of training."

***

There is more to the "Crop to Cup" story than a contract between interested parties that delivers a return to all. If that were all it was, it would be more than acceptable, but that would never be enough to satisfy Phillip Di Bella.

Perhaps this is one of the insights into why entrepreneurial intelligence enables some to stand out from the crowd.

In the contract between Di Bella Coffee and the coffee farmers there is a stipulation that crops must be grown and farmed under ethical and sustainable conditions. That of itself is not so remarkable. Today, many people talk about, and actively pursue, sustainable farming. However, I'm not sure that too many take this to the point where it becomes an all-consuming philosophy, one that not only helps define the business of Di Bella Coffee, but how that philosophy is applied. I'll leave it to Phillip Di Bella to paint the picture.

"I've never believed that the business of Di Bella is about coffee. I sincerely believe our business is about people. Every policy or protocol I have ever instigated in this company has emphasised that we are in the people business. From the way we work with our wholesale customers, to the protocols we implement to ensure that they can maximise their customer experience. The very description the 'ultimate coffee experience' means we are about coffee; that we deal in coffee. Of course we do, but more importantly the ultimate coffee experience is about how people understand and relate to that experience. It is our job – of every single person at Di Bella Coffee – to make sure that that experience is world class.

"If our brand is to be a relationship with our customers to ensure their loyalty and their repeat custom then we must put people first; they must be the focus of our decisions.

"It is our responsibility to support the people that support us, and to uphold our ethical responsibility as a company. That responsibility must start with the people who grow the beans, which are the very foundation of the ultimate coffee experience.

"All of the coffee roasted by Di Bella Coffee is sourced through our My Crop to Cup green bean buying program. Our own green bean specialist travels to coffee growing regions and deals directly with the growers who supply our coffee. Not only is that the best way for us to ensure that the highest quality crops are selected, it also means we are in a position to ensure that they are grown and farmed under ethical and sustainable conditions.

"The Crop to Cup philosophy is about building direct

relationships with coffee growing communities, and empowering them to work with us rather than for us to create the ultimate experience. We are determined to help coffee-growing communities reach their goals by working with them. This is not just altruism; this is good business sense. By taking an "educate, not dictate" approach we can work with farmers to identify opportunities and implement changes that will not only improve the quality of green beans but also the quality of life for those who produce them. If we can empower coffee-growing communities with what they need to realise their dreams, it's a win–win for everyone."

Phillip Di Bella's personal message is clear: "This is not about talking; it's about listening and acting.

"The Crop to Cup program was established in response to an appeal directly from the farmers to move towards a collaborative relationship with roasters and end users. Proactive roasters like ourselves embraced their appeal to open up channels of communication and support while, at the same time, allowing coffee growers to take ownership of their success and drive their own development.

"The support that the program provides goes beyond financial advantage. For the farmers, being part of the program is being a part of a team that cares not only about their crop, but their wellbeing as a business, as a community and as a people.

"Crop to Cup is committed to building skills locally, providing job security and growth opportunities for local workers, upholding fair practice and encouraging responsible farming. In developing areas of the world where unskilled workers have little or no choices, we choose coffee."

\*\*\*

One of the unfortunate by-products of the world we live in is an unhealthy liking for negative media. If the headline doesn't engage in over-the-top sensationalism then it will most likely be killed before it gets to the front page (what an apt analogy). Recently, Phillip was criticised through the media for allowing children to work on coffee plantations in South America, in an apparent conflict with his philosophy of ethical responsibility. Phillips' response was not to defend himself, but to point out two facts.

Firstly, he doesn't employ the people who work on the plantations, so the media needed to get its facts right. Secondly, and unfortunately, many of these children were often the primary breadwinner in the home. Without their income their families would struggle, but, as a result of commitments by coffee companies around the world, including the "My Crop to Cup" program, these same children were receiving an education that would otherwise be denied them.

The media accusation angered Phillip. Not, he points out, because of a wounded ego, but because the journalist in question missed the point completely. The vision Phillip had for Di Bella Coffee engaged with those children and the farmers in a way that was both practical and rational; an economically rational decision on the part of the company and a practical way of helping the growers and their families. Far from being guilty of exploiting cheap labour, Phillip understood that by articulating and implementing all the parts of his vision he could actually do something positive.

The media and their audience, Phillip believes, would have been far better served acknowledging the power of a well-articulated vision than trying to expose a perceived weakness simply for a headline.

# 21

# Where to begin?

The catalyst for this book is Phillip Di Bella. Without his openness, honesty and commitment it would never have been written. If you've stayed with us to this point in the journey you will also appreciate why the complete story of entrepreneurial intelligence could not be told without casting the net wider. In many instances I have used my own experiences and knowledge to establish a key fact or to support a stated position. In consultation with Phillip, I researched and observed a broad diversity of other entrepreneurs that we believe have set the standards for intelligent entrepreneurship. We looked outside the sphere of business to explore consistent rules of leadership, acknowledging that the formula of vision, passion and brand, supported by emotional intelligence, is not exclusive to the domain of the commercial marketplace.

To my mind, Phillip Di Bella embodies the key principles of entrepreneurial intelligence. His intellect is highly developed and his knowledge and skills sets are well tuned. It goes without saying that Griffith University would not bestow an adjunct professorship on a person who was not at the top of their field. That is not to say he hasn't made mistakes. Of course he has, and he willingly acknowledges them, but mistakes are how we learn, and no one should ever be frightened of making a mistake – as long as they do learn.

One of the most insightful lessons I have learnt from Phillip Di

Bella is about risk. Uninformed or misguided commentators point to entrepreneurs and deride them as risk takers. Researching this book has unearthed hundreds of articles and papers that would have you believe that neither government nor the community should trust entrepreneurs, because of the risks they take.

On the contrary, I have come to the firm conviction that by applying entrepreneurial intelligence, entrepreneurs aren't risk takers at all.

The fundamental premise of this book is that entrepreneurial intelligence is built on a simple, four-part formula of vision, passion, brand and emotional intelligence. As we have evolved the formula, we have debated the issue of nature versus nurture and have come to the conclusion that entrepreneurial intelligence is a combination of both. Both of these propositions are integral to my conviction that successful entrepreneurs aren't risk takers, and the clues can be found on every page of this book.

The Macquarie Dictionary defines 'risk taking' as the adoption of practices which are inherently dangerous. A risk taker is, therefore, someone who has such an inclination.

When I asked Phillip Di Bella if he was a risk taker, his response was blunt.

"Absolutely not."

He's absolutely right.

The very notion of entrepreneurial intelligence defies taking risks. Entrepreneurs like Phillip don't take risks with their money, or anyone else's for that matter. What they do is invest their money, their time and their energy in their vision, and they do so with passion and by building a solid foundation through their brand. That is not about risk, or risk taking, that is about having confidence in the direction you want to take, having the necessary commitment to stay the distance and ensuring you have a market-focused structure in place that can empower the resources you apply to the journey to make it happen.

Then entrepreneurial intelligence demands that successful entrepreneurs apply a level of emotional intelligence to their decision-making to ensure that their investment stays on track.

\*\*\*

What about the other entrepreneurs we've discussed in this book?

Did Bill Gates invest in his vision and passion, or did he take a risk? Was the late Steve Jobs risking his own funds and those of his investors, or was he investing in a vision that would revolutionise the way people viewed computers, a view that would open up a whole new dimension to engage with the digital world?

When Phillip Di Bella imagined a world where there could be an ultimate coffee experience, he imagined a world where someone had the capacity to influence every aspect of that experience.

Looking back, Cosmo was a microcosm of Phillip's future world, an invaluable insight into the potential power of his vision. It gave him the opportunity to learn everything there was to learn about a great coffee experience. He learnt where the pitfalls and dangers were, the strengths he would need to build on and the weaknesses he would need to eliminate. It opened up for him the world of coffee and an understanding of the enormous potential of the market opportunity for good coffee, let alone the ultimate coffee experience.

At the heart of the ultimate coffee experience is a great cup of coffee. At the heart of Phillip's success in applying the principles of entrepreneurial intelligence is his preparedness to invest in his vision, and to invest in his passion for learning and developing his own skills. He also understands the potential power of a brand strategy that can articulate what the Di Bella brand offers, and he has identified the steps and controls the brand needs to have in place to deliver on his promise.

Phillip Di Bella has not taken risks; Phillip Di Bella has invested in a formula, one that may not work for everyone, but which will work for those who are prepared to put the hard work in and who are prepared to take on-board advice from someone like Phillip, who has already been there:

> "Most people who start up a small business make the fundamental mistake of failing to identify whether there is a real opportunity in the market. Then they compound the problem by only doing some of the things they need to do, some of the time. Take coffee. Cosmo had great coffee but it had crap branding. Another group had crap coffee but got the branding right and tried to swing it with good service. Another group was just in it for the short haul and didn't do either very well. Instead of getting the product right all of them were obsessed with making money.
>
> "I never focused on making money. If you get all the parts of your business right, then money will come. My opportunity was to develop a company that offered amazing coffee through an amazing brand, and to do it consistently. So that's what we did."

I remember the conversation well. We were sitting in Phillip's office. I had just been served with my first flat white for the morning, having made an early start to beat the peak hour traffic. With a wry smile I suggested that he had summed up the book in two paragraphs.

He smiled back with a shake of his head.

> "Maybe, but for my money Lewis Carroll got it right when Alice asked the cat which way she should go and the cat responded by asking her where she was going. If Alice had known what her destination was, and if every budding entrepreneur out there knew where they were going, none of this – the book, the lectures I give, the seminars we run – none of it would be necessary. But she didn't, and the only

answer the cat could give her was the one he did – 'then it doesn't much matter which way you go!'

"You might have the greatest passion in the world, or the smartest brand strategy on the planet, but that will only get you some of the way. Even if you have more emotional intelligence than anyone else, that's not going to get you across the line if you don't have a clear vision of what you want to achieve and where you want to be."

# Author's note – Magic dust

*Entrepreneurial Intelligence* has been 2 years in the writing, and a lifetime in the making. For most of those 2 years it has been a labour of love, but there have been times when I would gladly have thrown the entire manuscript in the bin and walked away. I am sure Jann, my long-suffering wife, would have quietly rejoiced had I done so. It has been a complex gestation, one that was highlighted by Stephen Thompson when he was asked to confront the task of editing my nightmare of commas and colons. Oh, if only it had been that easy.

Writing this book was destined to be a complex task from the moment I first sat down with Phillip Di Bella. Phillip is a successful man, generous, but one who doesn't suffer fools gladly.

The first time we met was at a Di Bella Coffee planning session facilitated by an external consultant. I had been invited by a joint friend and confidante of Phillip's to provide some input on the Di Bella brand. As the session wore on I became increasingly frustrated at the direction (or lack of direction) it was taking. I sensed that Phillip was also struggling with the way the facilitator was handling things. I didn't know Phillip well enough to read the signs, but I decided I had nothing to lose by voicing my concerns.

I don't remember the exact words, but I challenged the outcomes achieved thus far. Phillip didn't say anything, but looked at me with a sense of expectation. I could also see other people around the table nodding. I suggested that perhaps we would achieve more from the time allocated if we considered a different structure. I briefly outlined the process I used to develop brand strategy, explaining my belief that using the brand to build strategy was more effective than traditional strategic planning because it placed the customer at the heart of all decisions.

That got Phillip's attention, because his entire mantra is customer driven and customer focused, and from that point on Phillip and I have shared a mutual respect that I hope is reflected throughout this book. Unfortunately, it also presented me with a dilemma.

Scattered throughout the book are instances where I have used the possessive 'we', followed not long after by the singular 'I' or 'me'. To some of you it may appear to be a small thing, almost tedious. To others it could appear to be a measure of confusion about who is actually writing this book; whether it is a collaboration by two authors, or me ghost writing on behalf of Phillip, or some other permutation entirely. To understand my dilemma you should understand how Phillip and I came to be collaborators in the first place, and how we approached the development of this book.

Not long after our first meeting, Phillip contracted me as a consultant to work with him and his team in the development of a brand strategy for Di Bella Coffee.

The Di Bella brand was already well-established and well-articulated. What Phillip wanted to ensure was that the Di Bella Coffee brand values were sustainable, and that as the organisation grew (as it was doing at a rapid rate), those values would continue to drive the company and be understood and applied by everyone in the organisation.

A number of planning sessions were scheduled, combining traditional strategic planning processes with customer-centric brand strategy principles. The resultant brand strategy that Phillip and his directors developed was an action plan that has steered the key pillars of Di Bella Coffee for the past three years. It is not a large file hiding at the bottom of someone's drawer but a living breathing strategic action plan that is at the heart of decisions taken on a daily basis, and which is reviewed every month at a meeting of the directors, and every year at a formal planning retreat.

The plan has also been a catalyst, and at times a linchpin to focus the company on its customers. It has provided a level of formality and discipline to the company's marketing endeavours, but it has never taken over from the entrepreneurial spirit that has been the true driver of success for Phillip Di Bella.

It is not surprising that this works, nor should it be surprising that Phillip Di Bella and I share many of the same values and hold true to the same principles. I have spent my entire working life focused on the customer and how to understand what goes on inside their heads. I have made a living from this skill both in my first career in the advertising business and, subsequently, through my passion in understanding brands and helping organisations develop strong brands.

In many ways, this was a learnt behaviour for me. I was fortunate enough to work with some of the most forward thinking companies in the world, who saw education and training as the cornerstone of their futures. When I left university, I took a cadetship with Myer, in their advertising department. A large slice of every week was spent in the company's classroom learning the essentials of retail marketing. Later on, I was fortunate enough to work with Ogilvy & Mather, who insisted that all their employees be engaged in ongoing learning, which they funded. I studied psychology through RMIT in Melbourne and marketing through the Business School at the University of Queensland. I also studied change management and group facilitation, amongst a raft of different disciplines, all undertaken to improve my skills in understanding people.

Phillip Di Bella spent his formative years studying customers in the best place he could – on the job. He demonstrated a natural and intuitive understanding of what customers did and didn't want. He constantly observed what was going on around him, and he has always demonstrated an insatiable thirst for knowledge. His appointment as an adjunct professor in entrepreneurship by

Griffith University is testament to the respect others have for his knowledge, and his ability to share that knowledge.

Phillip and I come from different generations and different backgrounds. We may not have a great deal in common, yet we share many of the same philosophies. What differs is the language we might use, or the descriptions we might give to different aspects of our beliefs. I will sit among an audience listening to Phillip speak and know exactly what he is going to say next; the point he is elaborating on and how he will conclude. I attend a monthly directors' meeting at Di Bella Coffee and find myself nodding at the point Phillip is making, and will then struggle to add something different when he prompts me for a comment. Nine times out of ten I finish up reinforcing the same premise or tenet, but talking about it from a different perspective.

I had previously collaborated with Dr John Harrison, from the University of Queensland, on a book we titled *Brand-aid*. It was first published in 2006 as a required text for Communication and Journalism students at UQ to explain the fundamental principles of branding. With John's co-operation I revised *Brand-aid* a few years ago to focus more on brand strategy. In the first instance, *Brand-aid* was a true example of collaboration, with both John and I sharing the writing after agreeing on the direction and our expectations for the book. For the revised publication, John allowed me to drive the re-write while he provided editorial support.

I gave a copy of the revised *Brand-aid* to Phillip Di Bella, who subsequently purchased copies to give to contacts and aspiring entrepreneurs. Copies of the book were used as giveaways at the Young Entrepreneurs events I outlined in the preface of this book. Clearly, Phillip found much in the book that was consistent with his own beliefs.

When Phillip had first discussed with me the possibility of writing a book, his primary motivation was to be able to capture his philosophies and principles in print. But I was reluctant to ghost write Phillip's story. I don't see myself as a writer, and certainly could never see myself living in someone's pocket with a tape recorder capturing every grisly detail. But the more we discussed the potential, a number of consistent themes and ideas began to emerge.

The four parts of the formula discussed in this book are very much part of Phillip's mantra. He constantly promotes the value of passion. It was one of the core values of an employee loyalty program he called PACII: Passion, Accountability, Consistency, Inspiration and Integrity. It is an integral part of the company's expected standards of behaviour contained in a document called *The Di Bella Way*. They are identified as essential for the company to achieve its vision through a passionate, dedicated, professional and enthusiastic workforce. In much the same way, vision is not just a word in Phillip's lexicon, it carries real meaning, and its value to Phillip, I believe, is accurately captured through that section of this book.

The more we discussed the components of the formula, the more excited we became about the potential of a book.

While Phillip was throwing ideas and concepts onto the table, I was applying the brakes. No matter what the book ultimately looked like, it would need to have a beginning, a middle and an end. It would have to tell a story and, hopefully, be entertaining enough for the reader to absorb the lessons being shared.

We agreed that people wouldn't read a boring book; they would not get drawn into something that didn't capture their imagination. We had already rejected the idea of a biography, and had agreed that I was the wrong person to become a ghost writer. In the end we agreed that the best way to tell the story was to interweave Phillip's experience with the key elements of the formula for entrepreneurial success. Phillip rejected any notion of editorial control and effectively handed responsibility for the direction and style to me.

So I went away to develop an outline for the book and to develop a process to capture the information required by identifying the key areas the book needed to cover, most of which had already emerged through our discussions. I also needed to prepare a list of interview questions that I could use to guide further discussions I would have to have with Phillip. And so evolved the style and content of the book, and the occasional confusion about 'we', 'I' and 'me'.

At the very heart of this book are the philosophies that Phillip Di Bella believes in. In some cases they have been given a slightly different cosmetic interpretation, but they have not been changed. As the author and researcher, I have also endeavoured to tell a story that is as far removed from dry, academic torture as I could. I have used my own experiences if I thought they added a different and worthwhile dimension. I have sought out other stories and researched the lives of a wide number of successful entrepreneurs to add colour to the narrative. Above all, I have tried to paint a picture of what Phillip and I agree is the basis of entrepreneurial intelligence.

# Index

Printed in Australia
AUOC02n0903170314
260255AU00007B/14/P

9 780975 816790